Beyond Civil Rights: Developing Economic, Social, and Cultural Rights in the UK

Sandy Ruxton and Razia Karim

Practical Action Publishing Ltd
25 Albert Street, Rugby, CV21 2SD, Warwickshire, UK
www.practicalactionpublishing.com

First published by Oxfam GB 2001
Converted to digital file 2010
Reprinted by Practical Action Publishing

© Oxfam GB 2001

Oxfam GB is registered as a charity in England and Wales (no. 202918) and Scotland (SCO 039042).
Oxfam GB is a member of Oxfam International.

Paperback ISBN: 9780855984748
PDF ISBN: 9780855986612

A catalogue record for this publication is available from the British Library.

All rights reserved. Reproduction, copy, transmission, or translation of any part of this publication may be made only under the following conditions:

- with the prior written permission of the publisher; or
- with a licence from the Copyright Licensing Agency Ltd., 90 Tottenham Court Road, London W1P 9HE, UK, or from another national licensing agency; or
- for quotation in a review of the work; or
- under the terms set out below.

This publication is copyright, but may be reproduced by any method without fee for teaching purposes, but not for resale. Formal permission is required for all such uses, but normally will be granted immediately. For copying in any other circumstances, or for re-use in other publications, or for translation or adaptation, prior written permission must be obtained from the publisher, and a fee may be payable.

Reasonable efforts have been made to publish reliable data and information, but the author and publisher cannot assume responsibility for the validity of all materials or for the consequences of their use.

The manufacturer's authorised representative in the EU for product safety is Lightning Source France, 1 Av. Johannes Gutenberg, 78310 Maurepas, France.
compliance@lightningsource.fr

Contents

Oxfam and JUSTICE iv

Preface v

Abbreviations and acronyms vi

Executive summary 1

1 Introduction 7

2 The nature of ESC rights and the historical development of human rights 11

3 The UK government's approach to ESC rights 21

4 The European framework for promoting and protecting ESC rights 29

5 The international framework for promoting and protecting ESC rights 37

6 Developing NGO advocacy on ESC rights: recommendations 46

Appendix:
Procedures and addresses for UN and ILO mechanisms 50

Glossary 53

Notes 56

Index 61

Oxfam and JUSTICE

Oxfam GB

Oxfam's UK Poverty Programme (UKPP) was created in the mid-1990s in response to the growth of poverty and inequality in the UK. The programme is guided by the same principles as Oxfam's work in other countries: it develops ways of working which enable people living in poverty to work out their own solutions and challenge the practices and policies that are responsible for creating and maintaining poverty. UKPP supports a wide range of groups, such as refugees and asylum seekers, single parents, and community organisations in impoverished neighbourhoods. For details, contact UK Poverty Programme, Oxfam House, 274 Banbury Road, Oxford OX2 7DZ. Tel. 01865 313105. E-mail gbpovertyprogramme@oxfam.org.uk

JUSTICE

JUSTICE is an all-party, legal human rights organisation which aims to improve British justice through law reform and policy work, publications, and training. It is the British section of the International Commission of Jurists. For details of JUSTICE's work, membership, and activities, contact JUSTICE, 59 Carter Lane, London EC4V 5AQ. Tel 020 7329 5100. Fax 020 7329 5055. E-mail: admin@justice.org.uk. Website: www.justice.org.uk

Preface

The UN High Commissioner for Human Rights, Mary Robinson, recently asserted that there is a strong link between poverty and the enjoyment of human rights:

'The reality of poverty is that the poor are denied almost all their human rights – the right to adequate housing, primary health care, education and food – not to mention the normal benefits of citizenship – fair legal treatment and access to justice, participation in the decisions that affect the poor, access to information and technology.' (Statement at the Special Dialogue on Poverty and the Enjoyment of Human Rights, Commission on Human Rights 56th Session, 12 April 2000)

While such comments often refer specifically to the desperate circumstances facing poor people in developing countries, rarely are they seen as relevant to those facing poverty, social exclusion, and discrimination in industrialised countries. Yet the denial of fundamental human rights which poverty represents also lies at the heart of poor people's experience in rich countries such as the UK.

The Human Rights Act 1998 is a milestone in the promotion of human rights in the UK. However, it primarily addresses civil and political rights. The well-established principle of the indivisibility of human rights demands that economic, social, and cultural rights (ESC rights) are guaranteed alongside civil and political rights. This report therefore sets out the case for using ESC rights as a framework for developing public policy in the UK, identifies the key international human rights instruments and how they can be used, and makes recommendations for developing a positive agenda.

The authors wish to thank the many individuals who have contributed to this Oxfam/JUSTICE project during its long period of gestation. At Oxfam, Audrey Bronstein, Fran Bennett, and Tricia Feeney all helped to guide the report and commented on drafts at various stages, and Ruth Emsley and Jodi Marshall helped to set up a seminar for NGOs to discuss interim findings. Catherine Robinson edited the text, and Kate Kilpatrick co-ordinated publication. At JUSTICE, Lib Peck provided ideas and additional information, Anne Owers made detailed comments and revisions, Zelah Senior and Frederica Donati assisted in the early stages of the project, and Ruth Allen co-ordinated the Oxfam/JUSTICE seminar. Beyond our organisations, four other people deserve particular thanks: Maggie Beirne, Gerison Lansdown, and Matthew Craven for commenting on an early draft, and Sian Lewis-Anthony for revising the text fully at a later stage.

Finally, we are also grateful to the wide range of NGOs who provided ideas and information throughout the project. In return, we hope that this study will provide them with a solid foundation for future joint work to advance ESC rights in the UK.

Sandy Ruxton
Razia Karim

October 2001

Abbreviations and acronyms

CEDAW:	Convention on the Elimination of Discrimination Against Women	EU:	European Union
CERD:	Convention on the Elimination of all Forms of Racial Discrimination	HRA:	Human Rights Act 1998
		ICCPR:	International Covenant on Civil and Political Rights
CESCR:	UN Committee on Economic, Social and Cultural Rights	ICESCR:	International Covenant on Economic, Social and Cultural Rights
CRC:	Convention on the Rights of the Child	ILO:	International Labour Organisation
CSA:	Child Support Agency		
ECHR:	European Convention on Human Rights	UDHR:	Universal Declaration of Human Rights
EctHR:	European Court of Human Rights	UNCRC:	UN Convention on the Rights of the Child
ECJ:	European Court of Justice		
ECOSOC:	United Nations Economic and Social Council		

(A fully annotated glossary is appended to the main text.)

Executive summary

Oxfam and JUSTICE: an approach to ESC rights

The enactment of the Human Rights Act 1998, and its implementation in October 2000, have made the idea of human rights fundamental to UK government and society. The Act requires a re-evaluation of the relationship between government and citizen. In placing the language of rights at the centre of our legal and political systems, it also presents an opportunity to further the protection of a wide range of rights, including those (such as many socio-economic rights) which are not included in the Human Rights Act.

Oxfam and JUSTICE believe that economic, social, and cultural rights (ESC rights) are an essential foundation of citizenship, alongside civil and political rights. Conversely, poverty and social exclusion are a denial of human rights, preventing people from exercising their full rights (such as the rights to housing, to health care, to education, to an adequate standard of living, and to social security). Moreover, living in persistent poverty and social exclusion denies individuals and families a full role as active participants in society.

In order to tackle these issues effectively in the United Kingdom, it is essential to develop public policy within a framework of ESC rights. This would be a crucial step towards ensuring that opportunities are available to all to participate in society on an equal basis.

Oxfam and JUSTICE believe therefore that non-government organisations (NGOs) should increasingly work within an ESC-rights framework. We welcome the implementation of the 1998 Human Rights Act and believe that it provides significant opportunities for NGOs to promote ESC rights. These opportunities should be fully exploited, and in addition, NGOs should lobby the UK government more actively to press for the adoption of a broader framework of ESC rights.

The potential of the Human Rights Act

On 2 October 2000, the Human Rights Act 1998 (HRA) came into force, incorporating the European Convention on Human Rights into UK law. The main effects of the Act are as follows.

- All people within the UK are now guaranteed positive civil and political rights.
- Individuals are now able to assert these rights in UK courts and tribunals.
- All public authorities have to ensure that their actions meet the standards of the Act, and they will be held accountable if they do not.
- The government must certify whether future legislation is compatible with the Act. Acts of Parliament remain supreme.
- The HRA will promote the development of a human rights culture in the UK.

The primary concern of the Human Rights Act is the provision of protection for 'civil and political rights', rather than ESC rights. Although we welcome the HRA, we believe that it does not guarantee a comprehensive statement of ESC rights – for example, the right to the highest attainable standard of health, and the right to a decent standard of living. Nevertheless, the distinction between the two sets of rights is often blurred in practice, and the HRA is likely to provide some opportunities for non-government organisations and others to lobby for the more effective implementation of

> 'For most British people human rights are synonymous with civil and political rights – the right to protest, freedom of religious worship, freedom from torture etc. One of the consequences of this has been to marginalise – in the public debate – economic and social rights, and to downplay their importance.'
>
> Foreign and Commonwealth Office, Human Rights Annual Report for 1999, Cm4404

> **Key findings of this report**
> - The Human Rights Act 1998 is welcome. While its main focus is upon civil and political rights, there is scope for the promotion of a limited number of ESC rights under the Act.
> - Although the UK government promotes ESC rights – and the interdependence of all rights – abroad, at home it tends to prefer instead a language and philosophy which emphasise individual responsibility more strongly than individual rights.
> - Recent developments in Northern Ireland, where the Human Rights Commission has set out a draft Bill of Rights which specifically includes ESC rights, may prove influential in debates in the rest of the UK.
> - It is sometimes thought that ESC rights are too vague or too political to be enforced in the courts, but this is not necessarily the case. Seemingly vague rights, such as the right to equality, can be and are justiciable. In addition to enforcement in the courts, full implementation of all ESC rights may require changes in public policy and thinking. It will not necessarily require high levels of additional resources.
> - The UK is party to a number of European and international treaties governing ESC rights. This fact provides opportunities to lobby for domestic implementation of ESC rights. There is evidence that, in practice, the UK falls short of certain of its international obligations under these treaties.
> - NGOs can use the 'non-discrimination' principle contained in all human rights treaties to secure protection for excluded groups. At EU level, new opportunities for promoting 'non-discrimination' exist.

ESC rights in the UK and the European Union (EU).

UK government ambivalence about ESC rights

The government has stressed the importance of the 'indivisibility' (i.e. the interdependence) of the whole family of rights – not just civil and political rights, but also economic, social, and cultural entitlements. Yet this emphasis is primarily visible within UK foreign policy, and has not been accorded similar prominence in relation to UK domestic policy.

Some ESC rights do enjoy protection in UK law, such as equal pay for work of equal value, the prohibition on discrimination in certain activities, and the national minimum wage. The law also protects entitlements to social security, to health and safety at work, to housing, and to education.

Nevertheless, social policy in Britain often prioritises individual responsibility over individual rights (for example, by imposing increasingly stringent eligibility tests for benefits). These responsibilities appear to be targeted disproportionately on poor and vulnerable sectors of society – the very groups most in need of a guaranteed set of economic, social, and cultural rights.

At European level, the UK has so far refused to ratify the revised Council of Europe Social Charter (the ESC equivalent of the European Convention on Human Rights (ECHR)) and its new complaints procedure – even though it has incorporated the ECHR into UK law through the Human Rights Act.

Can ESC rights be effectively enforced and implemented?

- Traditionally, ESC rights have been regarded as 'non-justiciable' (i.e. not capable of being decided in court). But ESC rights are often expressed in a manner no less precise than many civil and political rights. For example, the notion of an 'adequate' standard of living is open to interpretation, in the same way as the extent of the right to freedom of expression.
- It is also argued that ESC rights lack the 'absoluteness' that characterises civil and political rights (i.e. ESC rights vary over time and from place to place). Yet it is possible to identify a minimum core content for each ESC right. And conversely, civil and political rights have also changed over time (for example, in the areas of children's rights, the definition of what constitutes 'a family', and legislation on racial equality).

- It is sometimes claimed that ESC rights distort democracy, because their interpretation requires judges to make policy decisions. But examples from courts in other countries suggest that, in practice, judges do not usurp the roles and functions of politicians and policy makers.
- The argument is also advanced that it is easier to protect civil and political rights than ESC rights, because the latter require very considerable financial resources. But this distinction is not clear cut. For example, while it is true that the provision of a system of health care to ensure the right to the highest attainable standard of health demands huge resources, the same is true in respect of the right to a fair trial, which requires major investment in the provision of courts, judges, legal aid, and other types of infrastructure.

The key to understanding the implementation of ESC rights is the requirement under the International Covenant on Economic, Social and Cultural Rights (Article 2(1)) – ratified by the UK – that States should guarantee the 'progressive realisation' of ESC rights. 'Progressive realisation' requires States to take immediate steps towards the full implementation of ESC rights. However, at the same time, Article 2(2) of the Covenant provides that States must ensure that all ESC rights should be protected without discrimination on any of the prohibited grounds; this is an immediate obligation and not subject to the notion of progressive realisation.

The international and European legal frameworks

There is a range of international and European human rights instruments which promote ESC rights – either wholly or in part. These include the following:

- The Universal Declaration of Human Rights (1948) (UDHR)
- The International Covenant on Economic, Social and Cultural Rights (1966) (ICESCR)
- The Convention on the Elimination of Discrimination Against Women (1979) (CEDAW)
- The Convention on the Elimination of all forms of Racial Discrimination (1966) (CERD)
- The Convention on the Rights of the Child (1989) (CRC)
- Conventions of the International Labour Organisation
- The European Social Charter of the Council of Europe (1961, and 1988 Additional Protocol) and the 1996 Revised Social Charter.

The UK has ratified the above instruments (except for the 1988 Protocol to the Social Charter, and the 1996 Revised Social Charter) and is required in most cases to submit regular reports on progress in implementation to the relevant supervisory committees. However the instruments do not have domestic legal effect, because they have not been incorporated into UK law by an Act of Parliament. Nevertheless, they provide a useful means of assessing domestic law or policy against human rights standards and of lobbying for improved conditions for poor and marginalised members of society. They are yardsticks by which NGOs can hold government accountable and so encourage the promotion of ESC rights at the national level. In addition, they may prove useful as an aid to interpreting and developing domestic law. Moreover, the UK is required to submit reports under many of these instruments, detailing their compliance with them.

Implementing ESC rights under the HRA and anti-discrimination law

This report highlights some aspects of ESC rights that may be addressed by use of the HRA, as well as anti-discrimination law. The following are some examples:

- *Asylum*: Support 'in kind' for asylum seekers raises issues under Articles 8 (right to respect for private and family life) and 14 (prohibition of discrimination); the provision of 'no choice' accommodation raises issues under Article 8.
- *Legal aid:* The issue of whether legal aid is available (for example, in relation to some complex social-security matters) may be affected by Article 6 (right to a fair trial).
- *Imprisonment for fine default:* Magistrates' courts in particular use fines widely, many for relatively minor offences. Given that many of those who default on fines live on very low incomes, the use of imprisonment in such cases – even as a last resort – may well fall foul of the important ECHR principle that the

punishment must not be unreasonable in relation to the original offence.
- *Child support:* The Child Support Agency (CSA) may be challenged, on the basis that its activities infringe Article 6 (right to a fair trial) and Article 8 (right to family life).

Other examples may include discriminatory legislation on social security and tax; 'bind-over' orders on parents, to require them to take proper care of and exercise proper control over a child convicted of a criminal offence; conditions of detention; the education of children excluded from school; and the rationing of health care.

There is potential for advancing ESC rights by using anti-discrimination law. All human rights treaties provide for rights to be implemented and protected without discrimination. However, the non-discrimination provision included in the ECHR (and now incorporated into UK law by the HRA) is limited in its coverage. This is because it only prohibits discrimination in the enjoyment of the rights and freedoms guaranteed by the other provisions of the Convention. A new Protocol 12 to the ECHR has been drawn up to provide a much stronger and free-standing right to equality, but it is not yet clear that the UK will sign and ratify this, or make it part of the Human Rights Act.

There is no overarching statutory or constitutional right to equality in UK law. Nevertheless, apart from the HRA provisions, there is a framework of anti-discrimination legislation covering matters of race, sex, and disability.

At the EU level, there is much potential for NGOs to influence the future direction of law and policy. There is now EU competence to tackle discrimination on grounds other than sex (under Article 13). Two new directives have been adopted; the first governs discrimination on grounds of racial or ethnic origin and covers the fields of employment, social protection, social security, social advantage, education, and the supply of goods, services, and cultural facilities. The second governs discrimination on the grounds of racial or ethnic origin, religion or belief, disability, age and sexual orientation, in the field of employment only.

> In October 1997, Oxfam and JUSTICE co-ordinated a joint submission to the UN Committee on Economic, Social and Cultural Rights. A coalition of non-government organisations contributed to the submission, entitled 'Poverty Undermines Rights in the UK'. The coalition subsequently gave an oral presentation to the Committee, and the submission was highlighted in the UK media, enabling NGOs to raise current policy concerns and to draw attention to the existing international legal framework.

Recommendations: developing NGO advocacy on ESC rights

Oxfam and JUSTICE believe that NGOs have a vital role to play in promoting ESC rights in the UK and that they should further develop their activity, based on the core principle that poverty and social exclusion represent a denial of human rights. Such action should include the following measures.

1. Developing mechanisms for protection

- *Building on the Human Rights Act 1998:* NGOs have a significant role to play in working towards implementation of the Act, and promoting publicly the indivisibility, interdependence, and equality of all human rights. This could be furthered by litigation by way of test cases, as well as advocacy designed to influence key Ministers and officials, related Parliamentary groups, and relevant media and educational outlets.

- *Parliamentary Joint Human Rights Committee:* NGOs should seek to ensure that the Committee accords sufficient importance to the monitoring and implementation of ESC rights, which fall within its wider remit to consider and report on human rights within the UK.

- *Independent Human Rights Commission for the United Kingdom:* NGOs should campaign for the establishment of an independent Human Rights Commission, building on parallel developments in Northern Ireland.

- *Anti-discrimination law:* NGOs should use anti-discrimination law to improve the protection of the ESC rights of disadvantaged groups and should promote further legislative action to extend the coverage of existing laws. They should also press the government to ensure

that the directives are fully implemented in domestic legislation. Further, NGOs are in a key position to identify excluded persons who could lead test cases under the Human Rights Act 1998.
- *The European Union:* NGOs should engage in activities at the EU and domestic levels to pursue legislation or litigation seeking greater protection of ESC rights using EU law and mechanisms.

2. Promoting ratification of key economic, social, and cultural rights instruments

- *Council of Europe Revised European Social Charter and the Additional Protocol:* NGOs should call for the UK government to announce a timetable for full ratification of the 1996 Revised Social Charter and the 1995 Additional Protocol (which provides for a system of collective complaints).
- *ECHR Additional Protocol 12:* This Protocol, which will add a free-standing non-discrimination provision to the European Convention on Human Rights, was opened for signature and ratification in November 2000. NGOs should work with other groups to persuade the government to ratify and incorporate the Additional Protocol into domestic law.
- *Moving towards an Optional Protocol to the International Covenant on Economic, Social and Cultural Rights:* NGOs should encourage the UK government to take a more positive stance, and should continue to lobby the UN for the adoption of a draft Optional Protocol, which would establish a complaints procedure to the ICESCR.

3. Monitoring and supervision

- *Responding to UK government periodic reports:* NGOs should work together on the production of alternative NGO (or shadow) reports, in order to monitor the UK government's compliance with its international obligations under ESC-rights instruments.
- *Ensuring that UK government reports are disseminated and debated:* NGOs should seek to ensure that there are transparent and structured mechanisms for access by Parliament to UK government reports under ESC-rights instruments, and that such reports are made available promptly in appropriate formats (including on the government website) to all tiers of government, public bodies, NGOs, and libraries.

4. Encouraging reviews and harmonisation of domestic law and policy with international human rights standards

- *ESC-rights audits:* NGOs should use and promote key ESC rights instruments as a framework for developing policy and practice, both within and beyond their organisations. Such organisations will need to audit their existing policies and practice to ensure compliance.
- *'Adoption' of international instruments:* NGOs should formally adopt the Revised Social Charter and/or the ICESCR as an expression of their commitment to the principles, and then use these instruments as a tool to audit policy and practice. They should encourage public authorities to do the same.
- *Reviewing UK 'reservations' to ESC-rights instruments:* A detailed review should examine UK reservations to ICESCR, ICERD, CEDAW, and the European Social Charter.
- *Further action to assess UK compliance with ESC-rights instruments:* NGOs should argue that when the government is preparing a submission to the supervisory bodies of ESC-rights treaties, comprehensive reviews should be undertaken of UK domestic law and policy, to assess compliance with the relevant articles of these instruments.

5. Lobbying and dissemination of information and material

- *Dissemination of information to individuals and civil society:* NGOs should design appropriate strategies and materials for raising awareness among individuals and civil society (for example, schools, church groups, or special-interest groups) about ESC rights. NGOs should also encourage the development of education on human rights within the national curriculum (and especially as part of compulsory education on citizenship from 2002), and seek to ensure that such education stresses the indivisibility of human rights and the importance of ESC rights.
- *Developing continuing consultation between the UK government and NGOs on socio-economic and cultural rights:* NGOs should seek to establish

on-going mechanisms (possibly operating through a loose coalition) for engaging with the UK government and devolved administrations on ESC rights.

- *Promoting ESC rights in devolved administrations:* NGOs should ensure the mainstreaming of ESC rights within the administrations in Scotland, Wales, and Northern Ireland. It is important that NGOs should initiate UK-wide activities and links, and should build on the knowledge that is emerging from Scotland, Wales, and Northern Ireland.

- *Developing UK NGO activity in relation to the Council of Europe:* National NGOs should lobby key bodies within the Council of Europe – in conjunction with international organisations – for improved access and consultation rights under the European Social Charter supervision process.

1 Introduction

The importance of economic, social, and cultural rights

The implementation of the Human Rights Act represented a significant milestone in the promotion of human rights in the UK. For the first time, human rights standards are directly applicable and enforceable in UK law, and will be binding on government and public administration. They now inform the process of law making and decision taking, and are subject to enforcement in domestic courts and tribunals.

As it incorporates most of the provisions of the European Convention on Human Rights, the Act will have greatest impact upon the exercise of civil and political rights. However, it is inevitable that the rights guaranteed – for example, the rights to life and to freedom from inhuman and degrading treatment, the right to respect for one's home and private and family life, the rights to education and property – will also touch on economic, social, and cultural rights.

The introduction of the Act also raises questions about the nature, status, and implementation of other key human rights instruments. In relation to social and economic and cultural rights, these include the International Covenant on Economic, Social and Cultural Rights, the Social Charter of the Council of Europe, other more specific UN and ILO Conventions, and the European Union's Charter of Fundamental Rights.

The UK government's Annual Human Rights Report, published in 1999 by the Foreign and Commonwealth Office (FCO), stressed the importance of recognising the 'indivisibility' (i.e. the equal value) of the whole family of rights – not just civil and political rights, but also social and economic rights:

The achievement of social and economic rights is enhanced by progress in achieving civil and political rights. The commitment to a right to development – which draws together the social and economic rights laid down in the Universal Declaration – underlines a vital lesson: that we fail to honour the Universal Declaration and cannot claim to be upholders of human rights unless we commit ourselves to securing all rights for all people.[1]

This welcome defence of the principle of indivisibility confirms the government's stated commitment to the promotion of human rights. Indeed, in its third report, the FCO states that 'Securing full respect for human rights is not only an objective of foreign policy – it is also a central objective of this Government's domestic policy'.[2]

These statements endorse the UK's long-standing adherence to all the major international human rights instruments, including those relevant to ESC rights. If the UK government is to implement as well as promote its obligations under these instruments, it is timely to consider how economic, social, and cultural rights can be given greater prominence in domestic policy as well as foreign policy.

Poverty and social exclusion as a denial of fundamental human rights

Until relatively recently, the link between poverty, social exclusion, and the denial of human rights was rarely recognised. However, understanding has grown of the close interrelationship between these issues. At the international level, the UN General Assembly reaffirmed in 2001:

... that extreme poverty and exclusion from society constitute a violation of human dignity and that urgent national and international action is therefore required to eliminate them;

and

...that it is essential for States to foster participation by the poorest people in the decision-making process in the societies in which they live, in the promotion of human rights and in efforts to combat extreme poverty, and for people living in poverty and vulnerable groups to be empowered to organise themselves and to participate in all aspects of political, economic, and social life, in particular the planning and implementation of policies that affect them, thus enabling them to become genuine partners in development.[3]

Within the UK (and elsewhere in Europe), this approach has been forcefully promoted by ATD Fourth World, an international NGO with a long-standing rights-based approach to poverty: 'Torture, detention without trial or denial of freedom of speech are unquestionable human rights abuses. But poverty is also a violation of human rights because it prevents people exercising their full rights.'[4]

The majority of UK citizens have come to rely upon a certain level of security, based on solid foundations such as employment, health care, housing, and education. Furthermore, the available evidence suggests that in practice the public recognises the importance of these rights: one recent poll found that 96 per cent of UK citizens believe in the right to 'free medical treatment at the time of need', expressing the view that this provision should be enshrined in a Bill of Rights for the UK.[5] In Northern Ireland, an opinion survey for the Human Rights Commission indicated that well over 80 per cent of respondents supported the inclusion of rights in respect of health, housing, and employment in a Bill of Rights.[6]

Yet for those facing poverty and social exclusion, the predominant experience is one of insecurity, often transmitted from generation to generation. A recent survey revealed that in 1999, for example, 24 per cent of households in the United Kingdom lacked three or more necessities (items that more than half of the population believes 'all adults should be able to afford and which they should not have to do without') because they could not afford them, compared with 14 per cent in 1983. By the end of 1999, 26 per cent of the population were living in poverty, measured in terms of low income and multiple deprivation of necessities. In addition:

- roughly 9.5 million people in Britain today cannot afford adequate housing conditions;
- about 8 million cannot afford one or more essential household goods;
- almost 7.5 million people are too poor to engage in common social activities considered necessary by the majority of the population;
- about 2 million British children are deprived of at least two things they need;
- about 6.5 million adults lack essential items of clothing;
- around 4 million are not properly fed by today's standards;
- more than 10.5 million suffer from financial insecurity.[7]

In recent years, poverty and social exclusion have increasingly been seen as a denial of fundamental rights. For instance, the European Anti-Poverty Network has suggested as follows:

This is how those affected experience it themselves: they have no way of exercising those rights recognised in the Conventions and Charters signed up to by the Member States, to which the very great majority of their fellow-citizens have access, such as the right to housing, the right to health care, the right to an education giving essential basic knowledge, the right to community life ... The worse-off individuals and families are, the more of all their civil, political, economic, social and cultural rights they lose.[8]

There is considerable evidence to show that living in poverty and social exclusion denies individuals and families any role as active participants in society. Indeed, the normal channels through which people can be heard are in practice inaccessible to people in poverty.[9]

Social policies, both in the UK and internationally, have in the past often been developed purely as a means of satisfying particular needs, and have frequently been based on governments' top–down perceptions of what these are. In contrast, a rights-based approach assumes that individuals must be active agents in shaping such choices. And while a needs-based approach helps to identify the resource requirements of particular groups, a rights-based approach strengthens the ability of vulnerable groups to claim economic, political, and social resources.[10]

As Mary Robinson (the UN High Commissioner for Human Rights) has argued,[11] there are considerable advantages to a rights-based approach, in that it

- empowers individuals and communities by enhancing the human dimension of poverty-reduction strategies;
- empowers the poor by creating the conditions needed for popular participation in decision making;
- provides the framework for developing a multi-sectoral approach to poverty reduction; and
- helps to prevent the conditions that lead to poverty and social exclusion.

Challenging the notion of 'duties'

Ideas about ESC rights are closely linked to concepts of social justice – a value to which the UK government has repeatedly stated its commitment. But increasingly the notion of social justice is being replaced in official discourse with that of a new 'social contract' between the government and the public. Within this philosophical framework, the exercise of rights is conditional upon the citizen fulfilling certain responsibilities (such as to seek training or work if able; to support one's children and other family members; to save for retirement; and not to defraud the taxpayer).

The notion that rights must be balanced with responsibilities and the interests of the community is undisputed. However, there are fears that the government's approach places too much stress upon the responsibilities of individuals, especially those facing poverty and social exclusion. In reality, promoting the notion of individual duty can provide a rationale for excluding individuals from State support when they fail to meet the terms of the 'contract' set by the government. This can easily result in poor people being blamed for their poverty, reinvigorating the long-standing – and widely discredited – notion in UK social policy of the 'deserving' and 'undeserving' poor.

Rather than focusing attention on the behaviour of individuals, there is a strong argument – presented in this report – that it is essential to develop a framework of ESC rights for public policy in the UK. Given the persistent high levels of poverty and inequality in the UK, and the government's repeated commitment to tackling social exclusion and promoting human rights, such a framework, based on international human rights law, would provide both a solid rationale and effective mechanisms for responding to these problems.

Background to this report

In October 1997 JUSTICE and Oxfam co-ordinated a joint submission to the UN Committee on Economic, Social and Cultural Rights. A coalition of non-government organisations (NGOs) contributed to the submission, which was entitled 'Poverty Undermines Rights in the UK'.[12]

Encouraged by this positive experience, JUSTICE and Oxfam decided to undertake the current study in order to explore the potential for developing further activity on ESC rights in the UK. Both organisations continue to believe that there is considerable merit in seeking to analyse and respond to public policy – especially on core matters such as poverty and social exclusion – from the perspective of human rights.

The focus in this study is on the opportunities for NGOs to promote ESC rights. We recognise that other key stakeholders, such as trades unions, have played and continue to play an important role in securing protection for ESC rights. However, it is apparent that economic rights are better protected than social or cultural rights, and we consider that the NGO sector is best placed to influence social-welfare policy so that it becomes firmly rights-based. Greater collaboration between NGOs, trades unions, lawyers, and other interested groups is essential, however, for the development of an ESC-rights agenda. In part, this must involve a concerted attempt to bring together organisations working on civil and political rights with those working on ESC rights (see Box 1).

Aims and objectives

The overall aim of continuing work done by JUSTICE and Oxfam on these matters is to promote the establishment of a comprehensive human rights framework in the UK, one which addresses ESC rights alongside civil and political rights. In order to achieve this aim, JUSTICE and Oxfam support the following medium-term objectives:

- to assess and promote awareness of ESC rights;
- to identify mechanisms for securing the protection of ESC rights in the UK;
- to ensure that the incorporation of the European Convention on Human Rights into UK law leads to increased protection of all human rights;
- to build support for ESC rights among key sectors, and in particular NGOs.

This study therefore represents a first step in what is likely to be a long-term process. It sets out current contextual issues – historical, legal, and political – in relation to human rights (and ESC rights in particular), analyses arguments

> **Box 1**
>
> 'On the one hand, the civil and political realm, which has appropriated the language of "rights" for itself, has been stereotypically legal, expert, and highly specialised. On the other hand, the economic, social and cultural rights world did not use the term "rights", but focused on issues of participation, community development, and bottom-up approaches. There is much that each world can learn from each other. The civil and political realm should be learning to empower people and groups and putting its expertise to the service of people so that they become the agents of their own change. The economic, social, and cultural realm needs to use the language and concepts of rights, needs to evolve enforcement mechanisms parallel to those in the civil and political realm, and to be more rigorous and "legal" in its approach.'
>
> (Maggie Beirne, Committee for the Administration of Justice, 14 July 2000[13])

about the status of ESC rights, explores the existing range of relevant human rights instruments, and identifies possible approaches to establishing a UK framework which will be truly comprehensive.

Finally, the report presents a set of recommendations for the possible development of further NGO activity in the UK.

Structure of the report

Chapter 2 (on the nature of ESC rights and the historical development of human rights) identifies the characteristics of various types of rights and sets out the historical background to the development of ESC rights and the primacy in practice of civil and political rights. It also counters the central arguments that are expressed against initiatives to develop ESC rights. These are that ESC rights are 'non-justiciable' (i.e. unsuited for adjudication); that they distort democracy; and that they require substantial resources. This chapter also highlights the government's emphasis upon individual responsibilities rather than rights, and the effect of this on poor and marginalised groups. The section concludes that none of these arguments significantly undermines the case in favour of developing ESC rights in the UK.

Chapter 3 ('The UK government's approach to ESC rights') examines the position taken by the UK government in relation to ESC rights. It then identifies some of the tools for securing protection for ESC rights within the existing framework of the Human Rights Act 1998 and anti-discrimination legislation.

Chapter 4 ('The European framework for promoting and protecting ESC rights') examines the scope for NGO action within Europe.

Chapter 5 ('The international framework for promoting and protecting ESC rights') examines the scope for NGO action using international instruments.

Chapter 6 ('Recommendations') offers suggestions for possible NGO action, under the following headings:

- developing mechanisms for protection;
- promoting ratification of key ESC rights instruments;
- monitoring and supervision;
- reviewing and harmonising domestic law and policy with international standards;
- lobbying, dissemination of information, and dialogue.

2 The nature of ESC rights and the historical development of human rights

What are economic, social, and cultural rights?

ESC rights have been dubbed 'second-generation' rights. They have their roots in the growth of ideas about social justice in the nineteenth and twentieth centuries. The tag of 'first-generation' rights has been given to civil and political rights whose roots can be traced back to the eighteenth century.[14] The fact that ESC rights and civil and political rights have frequently been regarded as two distinct and separate categories of rights is due largely to an accident of history. Indeed, as outlined below, when the international community began to draft international human rights instruments after World War II, they did not at first differentiate between these groups of rights. However, the East–West divisions of the Cold War era led in practice to the separation of these rights, and the prioritisation, in the West, of civil and political rights. In this section we argue that, despite this fact, the two sets of rights are indivisible: that is, they form a single unified body of rights.

> **Box 2: Examples of economic, social, and cultural rights**
>
> - the right to work
> - the right to the highest attainable standard of health
> - the right to education
> - the right to an adequate standard of living
> - the right to social security

The historical development of ESC rights

The adoption by the UN General Assembly of the Universal Declaration of Human Rights (UDHR) on 10 December 1948 was a response to the atrocities of the 1930s and 1940s. It marked a watershed in the promotion of human rights at the international level. It also recognised the principle that States would be responsible for violations of human rights. The UDHR is an aspirational declaration which sets out a comprehensive range of human rights within a single text. It asserts the indivisibility and interdependence of all human rights and makes no distinction between civil, political, economic, social, or cultural rights.

Following the adoption of the UDHR, the UN General Assembly decided to give legal force to the rights contained in it. Consequently, the UN Commission on Human Rights began drafting a single human rights Covenant to impose on Member States legal obligations in respect of both civil and political rights and ESC rights. However, in the course of the drafting process, Cold War divisions resulted in the development of two separate covenants, with one covering civil and political rights, and the other ESC rights. Western States were suspicious of ESC rights, which they associated with socialism; civil and political rights, on the other hand, were perceived to be less problematic, having found domestic expression in a number of constitutions, including those of the USA and France. By separating the two sets of rights, it was then possible to secure different means by which they could be enforced. This will be discussed in more detail in Chapter 5.

The International Covenant on Civil and Political Rights (ICCPR) and the International Covenant on Economic, Social, and Cultural Rights (ICESCR) were completed in 1966 and entered into force in 1976. Together with the UDHR, these three instruments comprise what is known as the International Bill of Rights, which provides the international legal framework for the promotion and protection of all human rights.

It is worth noting that the Council of Europe[15] adopted a similar approach in relation to the two sets of rights by drafting two parallel instruments, namely the European Convention on Human Rights and the European Social Charter. These were completed in 1950 and 1963 respectively. They will be examined in Chapter 5.

The primacy of civil and political rights over ESC rights

International experience

Although the UN formally recognises the indivisibility and interdependence of all human rights, in practice in Western countries the language of civil and political rights has gained greater acceptance than ESC rights.

> **Box 3: Examples of civil and political rights**
>
> - the right to life
> - the right to a fair trial
> - the right to freedom of expression
> - prohibition against torture
> - the right to liberty and security
> - the right to freedom of religion and conscience

In general, treaties protecting civil and political rights have incorporated complaints mechanisms, enabling individuals alleging violations of their rights to submit petitions for adjudication. By contrast, treaties protecting ESC rights were accorded more restricted methods of supervision, namely monitoring of reports submitted to them by States Parties (i.e. those States that ratified the treaties). Thus, at the UN level, both the ICCPR and the ICESCR require States Parties to submit periodic reports to their respective treaty-monitoring bodies on measures taken to comply with the provisions of the Covenants. However, only the ICCPR has a complaints mechanism; a comparable procedure under the ICESCR is under consideration but has so far eluded agreement. As a consequence, while the ICCPR has generated a wealth of case law which interprets and gives life to its provisions, the ICESCR has not had the benefit of such a system.

The same is true at the European level. The highly developed and sophisticated right of individual petition under the European Convention on Human Rights, along with the jurisdiction of the European Court of Human Rights, has transformed international human rights law – largely in relation to civil and political rights. This contrasts sharply with the absence, until recently, of a complaints mechanism under the European Social Charter.

The growing body of UN, European, and inter-American case law has strengthened the position of civil and political rights within international human rights law. In the context of the UN and Europe and in the domestic law of some States, some protection for ESC rights has, however, been provided through the expansive interpretation of civil and political rights. As argued elsewhere in this report, the UK Human Rights Act 1998 is likely to have indirect but important implications for ESC rights.

> **Box 4**
>
> '... the combined values that have driven human rights thinking since the Second World War – liberty, justice, dignity, equality, community and now mutuality – inevitably lead to a concern with social and economic rights, whatever means of enforcement is adopted.'
>
> (Francesca Klug: *Values for a Godless Age: The Story of the United Kingdom's New Bill of Rights*[16])

National experience

The primacy of civil and political rights over ESC rights is reflected in the Constitutions and Bills of Rights of many Western countries. Recent examples include the New Zealand Bill of Rights 1988 and the Canadian Charter on Fundamental Rights and Freedoms, which guarantee constitutional protection for civil and political rights, but not for ESC rights.[17]

The position is very different elsewhere. There are some instances where constitutional provisions which appear designed exclusively to protect civil or political rights have been subjected to dynamic interpretations in order to include ESC rights. Thus in India, the Supreme Court has held that the right-to-life provision under the Constitution includes the rights to a livelihood and to education. Pressure has also been exerted by NGOs in a number of States (among them New Zealand, Canada, and Ireland) for inclusion of ESC rights in the Constitution. The South African Constitution, recently established to meet the challenges of the post-apartheid era, provides the best example of a constitution which deliberately sets out to protect ESC rights.

Although United Kingdom law does not provide comprehensive express protection for ESC rights at a constitutional level, some progress has been made, over the last decade, towards greater acceptance of notions of ESC rights. Thus, for example, a number of public authorities in the United Kingdom have formally adopted the UN Convention on the Rights of the Child (UNCRC). While placing those authorities under no legal obligations, the act of adoption has often led to the formulation of policies in keeping with the Convention's prescribed rights, thus securing, in practice, children's ESC rights as well as their civil and political rights.

Arguments for indivisibility

The distinction between the two sets of rights is not therefore intellectually or legally necessary or inevitable. In practice, the distinction has always been far from clear. Thus, almost every Western State has ratified the ICESCR, indicating wide-scale acceptance of the legitimacy of ESC rights. Furthermore, economic and social objectives have underpinned many progressive domestic reform programmes promoting social justice, including the New Deal programmes of Roosevelt in the USA and Mackenzie King in Canada during the 1930s, and the introduction of the welfare system in the UK in the late 1940s. In the years that followed the adoption of the two Covenants and, in particular, the years following the end of the Cold War, the justification for separating the two sets of rights became increasingly tenuous.

Arguments alleging the non-justiciability of ESC rights

Traditionally, it has been argued that ESC rights are not legal rights but mere aspirations, because they are not justiciable, that is, they are unsuited for adjudication. A number of arguments have been put forward in support of this view. However, on further examination, they do not provide valid reasons for arguing against the legitimacy of ESC rights as equal in status and importance to civil and political rights.

Box 5

'It is often argued against economic and social rights that these are abstract and collective notions, and not rights in the true sense. That argument must be rejected. Granted, the provisions of the European Social Charter are framed in general and, on many counts, seemingly vague terms. This is however not different from the case of civil and political rights.'

(Professor Stein Evju, Vice-President of the European Committee of Social Rights, addressing a conference in Belfast in 1999[18])

'ESC rights are vague and imprecisely defined'

An argument which held sway for many years was that in order to be legally enforceable, rights need to be precisely drafted. It was asserted that ESC rights were vague and imprecisely worded, and that this was necessarily the case, since the rights are aspirational and programmatic in nature. According to this view, courts of law are unable to convert abstract values such as the 'right to an adequate standard of living' into enforceable court orders. Civil and political rights, it was argued, are precisely drafted and accordingly more suited to adjudication.

In response it may be argued that ESC rights are no more vague and imprecise than some civil and political rights are. For example, the notion of 'adequacy' (as employed in Article 11 of the ICESCR, regarding the right to an adequate standard of living) is no more vague than that of 'fairness' or 'private life' (for example, the right to a fair trial and right to private life in Articles 14 and 17 respectively of the ICCPR).[19] Also, some ESC rights are clearly capable of having legal effect and in fact already enjoy protection in UK law, such as equal pay for work of equal value, the prohibition on discrimination in certain activities, and the national minimum wage. In addition, legal frameworks have been created to protect entitlements to social security, to health and safety at work, to housing, and to education: such entitlements are justiciable before Social Security tribunals, employment tribunals, and the civil courts.[20]

> Box 6
>
> 'What is certain is that many of the economic and social rights listed in the Universal Declaration are appropriate for enforcement by individuals, or better still by groups, in national courts ... States with advanced legal systems have experienced no difficulty in having courts and administrative tribunals deliver "distributive justice" in respect of both individual and group entitlements to housing and social services.'
>
> (Geoffrey Robertson: *Crimes Against Humanity*[21])

'ESC rights are variable in content'

It has also been asserted that ESC rights lack the essential characteristic of absoluteness, which is one of the hallmarks of human rights. It is said that they are variable in content, because they differ over time and from place to place, whereas civil and political rights are constant in their content and so are more susceptible to legal enforcement.

It cannot be denied that ESC rights are variable in content, since they depend on the resources and economic development of the State. However, it is possible to identify a minimum core content in respect of each ESC right, which imposes immediate obligations on all States Parties.[22] For example, the UN Committee on ESC Rights has stated that the term 'adequacy', in the context of the right to adequate housing contained in Article 11 of the ICESCR, is determined in part by social, economic, cultural, climactic, ecological, and other factors. Nevertheless, the right to adequate housing requires that *all*[23] persons should, among other things, possess a degree of security of tenure which guarantees them against forced eviction, harassment, and other threats. In addition, *all*[24] beneficiaries of the right to adequate housing should have sustainable access to natural and common resources, safe drinking water, energy for cooking, heating, lighting, sanitation, and other facilities.[25] Clearly, there is nothing vague about the Committee's language in respect of States' core obligations under the ICESCR. Similarly, in the EU context, common standards have been agreed through directives in relation to matters such as working hours and maternity leave. EU Directives, which must be implemented in all member States of the EU, have been the subject of much successful litigation, securing ESC entitlements for millions of EU citizens.

Furthermore, the notion of the absolute constancy of civil and political rights – or human rights in general — is illusory. There are clear examples of the way in which the content of civil and political rights has developed over time. Since the adoption of the 1989 UN Convention on the Rights of the Child, children's rights to participation in court or decision-making procedures that affect them (Article 12) have been increasingly acknowledged. Articles within the European Convention on Human Rights (ECHR) have been developed to reflect changing attitudes to corporal punishment and homo-sexuality, for example. Another specific instance relates to racial equality (see Box 7).

> Box 7: Changing notions of racial discrimination – a US example
>
> In the case of *Plessy v. Ferguson* 1896, the US Supreme Court upheld the doctrine of 'separate but equal' by stating that segregation was compatible with the 'equal protection' clause in the American Constitution as long as the facilities (such as separate railway carriages or schools) offered to white and black people were equal in nature. In 1954 the Supreme Court reversed that decision and held that segregation itself was a denial of the right to the equal protection of the law.[26]

It is also worth noting that the manner of implementation of civil and political rights will vary to some extent from one country to another. The concept of a fair trial, for example, may include an adversarial or inquisitorial system or the right to trial by jury in one jurisdiction, but not in another. However, the way in which the right to fair trial is guaranteed must not impair the very essence of the right. This reality is reflected, for example, in the endorsement by the European Court of Human Rights of the principle of the 'margin of appreciation' (the limited flexibility which the Court allows to States to implement rights in ways which are compatible with their own law and society, and which do not impair the essence of the right concerned). So even in relation to civil and political rights, variable practice, to a limited extent, is allowed, as long as the right itself is not undermined.

'ESC rights distort democracy'[27]

A major obstacle to the development of ESC rights as legal rights is the belief that it would be constitutionally inappropriate and undemocratic for judges to make policy decisions. The opponents of justiciability argue that ESC rights are programmatic and policy-driven, and that as such they require government action and resources; politicians should not be constrained in their scope for allocating such resources. Yet the protection of ESC rights does not require politicians to give up all their discretion, but it does require them to guarantee to everyone a minimum standard of social justice. Many countries, including the UK, have already accepted this principle by implementing laws on such matters as a national minimum wage and old-age pensions.[28]

Moreover, as will be seen, judges in most jurisdictions do from time to time make decisions affecting the distribution of resources, whether in the context of ESC rights or otherwise. In those cases, there is no question that the democratically elected parliaments retain sovereignty over policy and budget allocations. What is generally at stake for courts are issues such as fairness and equality, rather than the policies themselves.

The argument that ESC rights distort democracy was the principal reason behind the decision to exclude enforceable and comprehensive guarantees of ESC rights from the Irish Constitution when it was reviewed in 1995/96. The Review Group on the Constitution considered, in its report published in May 1996, that judicial activism in the development of the contents of rights was an encroachment on democracy and on the powers and function of Parliament. The Report further stated:

[social and economic entitlements] ... are essentially political matters which in a democracy it should be the responsibility of the elected representatives of the people to address and determine. It would be a distortion of democracy to transfer decisions on major issues of policy and practicality from the Government and the Oireachtas, elected to represent the people and do their will, to an unelected judiciary.[29]

The Report was criticised by the Irish Commission for Justice and Peace[30] in its own Report, 'Re-righting the Constitution'.[31] The Commission observed as follows:

The insertion of socio-economic rights in the Constitution could be effected only by the decision of the people through a referendum. This would confer a mandate at least as democratic as a decision of the Oireachtas. In the context of Ireland it would be no more difficult than interpreting rights already stated in the Constitution which include education and property rights.

The Irish Constitution, like the ECHR, does already provide for some ESC rights, including the right to education (Article 42) and to private ownership of property (Article 43). Somewhat like the Indian Constitution, the Irish Constitution (Article 45) also contains non-justiciable 'directive principles of social policy', although they have not been used so much by the Irish courts as by the Indian courts. These principles include the right to earn a livelihood, and a 'pledge' on the part of the State 'to safeguard with especial care the economic interests of the weaker sections of the community' and to contribute to their support. In general the approach of the courts to this Article has, however, been cautious.[32]

In practice, courts in other jurisdictions with competence in respect of ESC rights have shown great restraint when faced with questions which carry resource-related implications. The Constitutional Court in South Africa is charged with the protection of certain ESC rights, such as the right to emergency health care. In the Soobramoney case (see Box 8), it did not find that this right was non-justiciable, nor did it decline jurisdiction to hear the case on the grounds of lack of competence: the court simply took the view that there had been no violation of the constitutional right to emergency health care. But even in this limited circumstance the Court did not regard itself as being qualified to make detailed decisions regarding the equitable allocation of limited resources, and was careful not to usurp the role and function of political organs and service providers.[33]

In another recent South African Constitutional Court judgement, concerning the admission of foreign life-partners of gay South Africans on an equal basis with married South Africans, the Court found that 'writing in' words into a statute should interfere with the laws adopted by the legislature as little as possible and should not result in an unsupportable budgetary intrusion. 'Writing in' in this case had 'minuscule budgetary implications'.[34] On the question of parliamentary sovereignty, the Court noted that Parliament retained the power to amend the words which the Court had utilised.

> **Box 8: The justiciability of ESC rights in South Africa**
>
> The South African Constitution provides for a number of ESC rights which are capable of judicial determination, for example labour rights (Article 23); a right of access to adequate housing (Article 26); the right of access to food, water, and social security (Article 27); the right of access to emergency health care and a qualified right to other health care, subject to resources (Article 27); and the right to education (Article 29).
>
> In the case of *Soobramoney v. Minister of Health, KwaZulu Natal*,[35] the South African Constitutional Court had to determine whether a patient with a terminal illness had an automatic right to dialysis treatment under the right of access to emergency health care. The plaintiff argued that without dialysis he would need emergency treatment. This case clearly involved the distribution of insufficient resources, as dialysis treatment was available only to a limited number of hospitals and patients who satisfied certain criteria, due to its cost. The Constitutional Court dismissed the plaintiff's appeal, and in so doing it held that 'A court will be slow to interfere with rational decisions taken in good faith by the political organs and medical authorities whose responsibility it is to deal with such matters.'[36]

> **Box 9: The development of ESC rights in India**
>
> The Indian Constitution distinguishes between guaranteed judicially enforceable civil and political rights ('Fundamental Rights') and social and economic objectives which take the form of Directive Principles. The Directive Principles are not judicially enforceable. However, the Supreme Court has interpreted the fundamental rights in the light of the Directive Principles. The result has been an expansive interpretation of civil and political rights to include ESC rights; for example the right to life has been interpreted by the Court to include the right to health care,[37] to a livelihood,[38] to education,[39] and to a healthy environment.[40] Here, the Supreme Court has not felt itself constrained by constitutional competence or legitimacy to adjudicate on social and economic issues.

'ESC rights cost money'

The cost of implementing ESC rights has been another important and persuasive argument against their development as legally enforceable human rights. According to this approach, ESC rights are 'positive rights', whose implementation requires State action; this is costly, because it imposes an obligation on the State to make provisions for facilities such as housing, health care, and social security. By contrast, civil and political rights are 'negative rights', which require the State to refrain from acting: their implementation is regarded as free or inexpensive.

However, these arguments are misleading. It is now generally accepted that all human rights impose positive and negative duties on the State, amounting to a multi-layered obligation to respect, protect, promote, and fulfil all human rights.[41] (See Box 10.)

It is also a myth that civil and political rights are inexpensive to implement. For example, Article 3 of the ECHR entails a positive obligation to protect victims and potential victims of crime and abuse: an obligation which necessitates the expenditure of resources on policing, social services, and the prosecution process. Similarly, the concept of a fair trial includes the provision of free legal advice for those charged with a criminal offence, if they cannot afford legal representation. The Irish Review Group[42] proposed that the right of access to the courts should be included in the Constitution, and it accepted that this would involve the provision of resources to fund a comprehensive programme of legal aid.[43] More recently, the Northern Ireland Human Rights Commission has argued in similar terms (see Box 11).

In addition, the European Court of Human Rights has increasingly taken the view that rights traditionally regarded as requiring only that the State abstain from interfering, such as the right to freedom of expression, may also impose obligations on the State. In a case concerning a newspaper company whose employees and distributors had been systematically harassed, attacked, and in some cases killed, the Court held that the State had an obligation to conduct a thorough investigation into the criminal activities. In addition, the State was obliged to provide the newspaper with protection against unlawful acts of violence. Such an obligation would inevitably involve significant expenditure.[44]

> **Box 10: The multi-layered obligations of the State**
>
> Human rights have traditionally been divided between civil and political rights, which are said to be negative rights, and ESC rights, which are described as positive rights. The former do not require action by the State, whereas the latter do. However, it is now accepted that States are under a duty to *respect, protect, promote, and fulfil* all human rights – and these include positive and negative duties.
>
> The primary duty, to *respect* rights, requires the State to refrain from unjustified interference with the enjoyment of a right. In the context of the right to housing, for example, the State has a duty to refrain from arbitrary evictions. This does not require a commitment of resources by the State.
>
> The secondary duty, to *protect* rights, requires the State to implement laws and regulations. The obligation is to provide a legal framework, but not necessarily resources. Again, in the context of the right to housing this may include statutory protection from arbitrary eviction, harassment, and other threats by third parties. In civil and political rights it may, for example, include a statutory framework for the treatment and questioning of suspects held in detention.
>
> The tertiary duty, to *promote and fulfil* rights, does require positive action by the State, but the scope of the duty may depend on the precise formulation of the right. For example, the qualified right of access to adequate housing in the South African Constitution does not impose an obligation on the State to provide individuals with free housing; but it does place a duty on the State to assist individuals to realise this right through the provision of home loans or subsidies for low-income families. The unqualified right to education, by contrast, places an immediate duty on the State to provide free primary schooling. There is also a growing body of Strasbourg jurisprudence recognising that States have positive obligations in respect of rights guaranteed by the ECHR.

Lack of resources has not prevented some poorer States, such as South Africa and India, from implementing ESC rights. Other States which provide for ESC rights, either in the Constitution or as objectives in Directive Principles, include the Philippines, Namibia, Nigeria, the Republic of Ireland, France, and Italy. Most recently, Brazilian officials and NGOs have agreed on a redefinition of human rights, now broadened to encompass ESC rights in the framework of the government's National Human Rights Programme.

The South African experience presents a good example of how to implement ESC rights in a State with limited resources. The Constitution distinguishes between *qualified* and *unqualified* rights. The qualified rights are 'rights of access' to entitlements, for example the right of access to health care or adequate housing. The State is allowed to implement qualified rights 'progressively' and 'within available resources'. Other rights, such as the rights to basic education and emergency health care, and children's socio-economic rights, are not qualified by the 'access to' provision and they must be implemented without delay.

> **Box 11**
>
> '...the protection of civil and political rights also costs money and requires positive action. If people are not to be arbitrarily arrested, the police have to be properly trained. If trials are to be fair, the state has to provide legal representation for accused people who cannot afford to pay for their own lawyer. And if free speech is to be protected, the state must make a legal remedy available for those whose right is denied. If a state is to prevent torture, it will have to take a variety of positive steps to ensure that it never takes place. So the argument about public expenditure is not very convincing.'
>
> (Northern Ireland Human Rights Commission, (2000), Social and Economic Rights, www.nihrc.org)

Progressive realisation of ESC rights and core rights

The key to understanding ESC rights lies in Article 2 of the ICESCR. This Article provides as follows:

1. Each State Party to the present Covenant undertakes to take steps individually and through international assistance and co-operation, especially economic and technical, to the maximum of its available resources, with a view to achieving progressively the full realisation of the rights recognised in the present Covenant by all appropriate means, including particularly the adoption of legislative measures.

2. The States Parties to the present Covenant undertake to guarantee that the rights enunciated in the present Covenant will be exercised without discrimination of any kind as to race, colour, sex, language, religion, political or other opinion, national or social origin, property, birth or other status.

Article 2(1) sets out the basic concept of 'progressive realisation', which has been further developed by the UN Committee on Economic, Social and Cultural Rights (CESCR), the Limburg Principles on the Implementation of the ICESCR,[45] and the Maastricht Guidelines on Violations of ESC Rights.[46] The Limburg Principles, and the Maastricht Guidelines, drafted by groups of experts, offer contemporary interpretations of the treaty obligations. While not binding, these documents are regarded as authoritative interpretations of the ICESCR and are invaluable for an understanding of such notions as progressive implementation. Similarly, other international treaties which protect ESC rights may provide excellent guides to the interpretation of the rights secured in the Covenant.

Both the Committee and the Principles recognise that the concept of progressive implementation is flexible enough to allow for differences among States Parties and, more importantly, that full realisation will generally not be achieved within a short time.[47] However, the Committee has stated that the notion of progressive realisation could not be used by States as an excuse for deferring their obligations indefinitely. The obligation to take steps is one that States must honour within a short time after ratifying the ICESCR.

Furthermore, while the idea of progressive realisation of ESC rights takes account of the economic realities prevailing in a particular country, the Committee has stated that States have, under the ICESCR, 'a minimum core obligation to ensure the satisfaction of, at the very least, minimum essential levels of each of the rights'.[48]

The Committee goes on to state that if a significant number of individuals in a State are deprived of essential foodstuffs, or of essential primary health care, basic shelter or housing, or the most basic forms of education, then that State would be in violation of the ICESCR. The Maastricht Guidelines confirm the notion of minimum obligations owed by every State: 'resource scarcity does not relieve states of certain minimum obligations in respect of the implementation of ESC rights'.[49]

The core entitlements of ESC rights are accordingly not subject to progressive implementation; they apply 'irrespective of the resources of the country concerned or any other factors or difficulties'.[50] It should also be noted that the prohibition against discrimination contained in the ICESCR is not subject to progressive realisation: it is an immediate obligation incumbent upon States. Accordingly, all persons must be able to exercise their rights without discrimination. If ESC rights are accorded to one group and not to another, without any objective justification, the responsibility of the State is engaged under the ICESCR. In other words, the State has violated the Covenant.

Political opposition to ESC rights: rights over responsibilities?

During the past decade, the view that citizens have 'too many rights and not enough responsibilities' gained currency, especially in the UK.[51] Similarly, it is often argued that international human rights law accords insufficient attention to responsibilities. Until the late 1990s, this objection was employed to hinder the direct enforcement of any rights within the UK. (Since 1997, under two successive Labour governments, the same argument has been used to justify any proposed extension of rights.) Such views are ill-informed, however: international human rights standards are suffused with references not only to individual responsibilities, but also to the duty to consider the rights of others, which may take precedence.[52] For example, Article 29(1) of the Universal Declaration of Human Rights states that 'Everyone has duties to the community in which alone the free and full development of his personality is possible'. And the preamble to both the ICCPR and the ICESCR sets out that '...the individual, having duties to other individuals and to the community in which he belongs, is under a responsibility to strive for the promotion and observance of the rights recognised in the present Covenant'. This language makes clear that the individual has duties both to the community and to other individuals.

The emphasis on duty is also carried through into other human rights conventions. In the 1989 UN Convention on the Rights of the Child, for instance, Article 18(1) recognises that the basic responsibility for a child's upbringing rests on the parents. Article 27(2) recognises the parents' duty to provide for the child, and Article 5 the responsibility of parents to help the child in the exercise of his or her rights. Moreover, although some rights (such as the right to life or protection against torture) are stated in absolute terms in human rights law, there are restrictions on other rights, such as the right to a private life, or the right to freedom of expression, on such grounds as 'public morality', or 'to protect the freedoms of others', or 'public health'. In other words, human rights agreements do place some limits on the rights that they protect; they do not promote – as some have argued – 'unrestricted freedom' or rights without responsibility.[53]

Despite this subtle balancing of rights and responsibilities in international human rights law, the UK government has increasingly emphasised the centrality of 'duties' across a range of public-policy areas.[54] Relevant policy initiatives have included compulsory and stringent eligibility tests for social-security benefits; strengthening the emphasis on 'parental responsibility' in relation to families; encouraging the formulation of home–school contracts; and measures to address 'anti-social' behaviour. A more recent proposal is to withdraw benefits from offenders who do not comply with court orders. Overall such a programme amounts to a radical redefinition of the notion of social citizenship.

Although it is often promoted as a common-sense approach, the 'duties and responsibilities' principle inhibits the development of economic and social rights. For example, the UK government's emphasis on responsibilities appears to be targeted disproportionately on poor and vulnerable groups – those most in need of a set of guaranteed economic and social rights. Promoting the duty of the individual provides a rationale for withdrawing welfare entitlements from certain individuals. Such exclusion can then be justified as the fault of the individuals concerned, rather than the State – an approach with a long tradition in the UK, going back at least as far as the 1834 Poor Law. Meanwhile the occupational and fiscal benefits received by the majority of UK citizens carry no such obligations. The underlying difference in approach appears to undermine the central concept in human rights law: that of the equal worth of all citizens.

> **Box 12**
>
> '... the actions that the government had the right to expect from the poorest members of society appeared much more clearly than its responsibilities to them. Most of the participants in the APPG had little problem with the notion that rights and responsibilities should be in balance. Rather, it was the perceived imbalance between these concepts in the government's thinking that caused concern.'
>
> (First report of the All Party Parliamentary Group on Poverty[55])

Furthermore, increasing stress on individual responsibilities obscures the importance of economic and social rights. For instance, a 1998 government Green Paper on welfare reform[56] argues that 'at the heart of the modern welfare state will be a new contract between the citizen and the Government, based on responsibilities and rights'. Yet beneath this text is a two-column table, setting out the 'Duty of Government' (for example, 'to provide people with the assistance they need to find work'; 'to make work pay') alongside the 'Duty of Individuals' (for instance, 'to seek training or work where able to do so'; 'to take up the opportunity to be independent if able to do so'; 'to give support, financial or otherwise, to their children and other family members'; to 'save for retirement where possible'; and 'not to defraud the taxpayer').

Although the 'Duties of Government' are set out in the Green Paper, the terms of the 'contract' are defined by the government itself and are not negotiable. They also avoid any specific commitments and are, except in certain limited cases, not legally enforceable. Conversely, if individuals fail to meet their duties (for example, to take up work opportunities), they may in many cases be penalised by the State (for instance, by withdrawal of benefit entitlement); or in extreme cases their duties can be enforced through the courts. In other words, the 'contract', a legal term which implies genuine consent and reciprocity, in reality may be a means of reducing the role of the State and may thereby diminish the economic and social rights of the individual.

Finally, the notion of a contract between State and citizen, balancing the duties of government and individuals, may also downgrade the importance of addressing the responsibilities of a range of increasingly powerful actors in society, including large multi-national companies, media interests, and significant political or religious movements. Despite the growing influence of these actors on many aspects of the community, including the delivery of welfare services, debate about their responsibilities to society receives far less prominence than the notion of the responsibilities of the individual citizen. Moreover, corporations and businesses are themselves able to assert rights via the Human Rights Act, without necessarily acquiring any responsibilities towards those whose ESC rights are directly affected by their activities: for example, when company mergers result in asset-stripping and unemployment.

Summary

ESC rights have traditionally been accorded lower status than civil and political rights. However, the drafters of the Universal Declaration of Human Rights, the document generally regarded as the foundation stone of international human rights law, recognised the indivisibility of the two families of rights. Since the end of the Cold War era, there has been a growing acceptance of the concept of indivisibility. There is certainly far less reluctance to regard ESC rights as legal rights, and an increasing commitment to providing means of redress for violations of ESC rights.

3 The UK government's approach to ESC rights

This chapter compares the UK government's approach to ESC rights at the international, European, and national levels. It then explores how ESC rights might be implemented within the UK, in the light of the Human Rights Act and anti-discrimination law, and options for developing related NGO advocacy.[57]

> Box 13
>
> 'Human rights are indeed of little value without freedom from hunger, from want and from disease. And economic and social rights are as important as civil and political rights.' (Robin Cook, former Foreign Secretary[58])
>
> 'The Declaration is very clear that human rights mean not just civil and political, but also cultural, economic and social rights. Not just freedom from fear but freedom from want ... I'm not asking for more emphasis on social and economic rights and less on civil and political, but a balance that seeks to secure all rights for all people.'
>
> (Clare Short, Secretary of State for International Development[59])

The UK's international and domestic perspectives compared

Although the UK government has promoted the indivisibility of rights in overseas contexts, it has not promoted this idea domestically, where the emphasis has been on concepts of civil and political rights. In a series of recent speeches, government ministers with foreign-policy responsibilities have repeatedly highlighted the importance of economic and social rights alongside civil and political rights (see Box 13), yet this emphasis is lacking from speeches by ministers with domestic responsibilities. The Foreign Office/DFID 2000 Annual Report on Human Rights devotes an entire chapter to 'Economic and Social Rights', and goes on to argue:

To many people, human rights mean only civil and political rights – freedom from torture, the right to equal and fair treatment, freedom of opinion and expression.[60]

The 1999 Report suggested:

One of the consequences of this has been to marginalise – in the public debate – economic and social rights, and to downplay their importance.[61]

The 2000 report states:

Human rights mean not just freedom from fear, but also freedom from want. That is why the Government is committed to promoting all human rights – economic, social and cultural, as well as civil and political.[62]

Further, the government's second development White Paper, 'Eliminating World Poverty: Making Globalisation Work for the Poor' (2000), commits it to a rights-based approach to development which allows people to speak for themselves, to advance their own interests, and to realise their human rights. An example of how this approach is being applied in practice is Britain's active support for the enshrining of ESC rights in the Kenyan Constitution.[63] Yet at home there is a strong tendency, in the context of public policy, to focus on promoting 'welfare' rather than 'rights'.

The UK government's approach to ESC rights at the European level

The UK government's approach to ESC rights at the European level is also somewhat ambivalent. On the one hand, it has accepted the EU's competence in respect of policy-making on social issues, which had previously been contained in a Protocol to which the UK (under the most recent Conservative administration) failed to adhere. This acceptance has led to limited, but significant, advances in economic and social rights for UK workers (such as regulation of working time, and improvement of working conditions and leave arrangements).

> **Box 14**
>
> 'The principle of the indivisibility of human rights is a keystone of EU policy. This means that ESC rights should be accorded as much importance as civil and political rights. This principle not only reflects the doctrine embodied in both the Universal Declaration of Human Rights and the Council of Europe's human rights regime but also the consensus on the importance of the European social model. However, the Union's commitment has hardly been matched by its practice. This is true in both the internal and external dimensions of EU policy.'
>
> P. Alston and J.H.H. Weiler (1998) 'The European Union and Human Rights: Final project report on an agenda for the year 2000', European University Institute.

On the other hand, the UK government took a cautious approach towards the development of the EU Charter of Fundamental Rights (which includes some ESC rights as well as civil and political rights), supporting it as a 'showcase of rights', but opposing any suggestion that it should impose binding legal obligations.

Within the Council of Europe, the UK has also been reluctant to embrace fully the ESC rights that are provided. Although it ratified the 1961 European Social Charter (the ESC equivalent of the ECHR), it has not so far ratified the wider-ranging 'Revised European Social Charter' issued in 1996,[64] unlike most other European governments. However, despite the fact that the European Social Charter was missing from the government's 1999 review of the UK's obligations under international human rights treaties, the government does appear to be moving on the issue. The FCO's 'Human Rights Annual Report' for 2000 states that the government will ratify it 'in due course'.

ESC rights under devolution: the Northern Ireland experience

There are significant differences within the constituent parts of the UK in the approach adopted towards the full family of human rights. The position in Northern Ireland deserves particular attention in this regard. While it is not government policy to promote ESC rights in other parts of the UK, it has expressly encouraged the promotion of such rights in Northern Ireland. The Good Friday Agreement, signed in Belfast in 1998, seeks to ensure 'rigorous impartiality on behalf of all the people in the diversity of their identities and traditions [which] shall be founded on the principles of *full respect for, and equality of, civil, political, social and cultural rights*, of freedom from discrimination for all citizens, and of parity of esteem and of just and equal treatment for the identity, ethos and aspirations of both communities' (our italics).

The Agreement also provided for the creation of a Northern Ireland Human Rights Commission to promote and protect the full range of human rights, including ESC rights. To meet its responsibilities in relation to ESC rights, the Commission has, for example, already submitted evidence to the European Social Rights Committee (the supervisory body monitoring the Council of Europe's 'European Social Charter'), outlining its concerns at failures to protect ESC rights adequately in Northern Ireland (for example in the areas of housing, community care, and health services).

Another central task of the Commission is to make recommendations on what should be contained in a Bill of Rights for Northern Ireland. The Bill will make provision for the protection of rights that are not already guaranteed under the European Convention on Human Rights. In relation to ESC rights, the Commission has argued that the rights to health care, an adequate standard of living, housing, access to work, and a healthy and sustainable environment are suitable for inclusion in the Bill of Rights.

In addition, the Commission has recommended that a general clause to govern interpretation of economic and social rights should be included within the Bill (see Box 15). It would mean that individuals and groups would not be entitled to specified standards of health care, particular forms of housing or a particular form of work-related training; however, they could challenge any failure by a government department or public body to take reasonable or proportionate steps to deliver ESC rights. The courts would not be able to take direct decisions on how to allocate resources (beyond perhaps specifying certain minimum standards which must always be met), but would be able to supervise the proper implementation of the rights in question by applying concepts such as proportionality, reasonableness, equality, and human dignity. The implementation mechanism would be modelled on the current Human Rights Act 1998 so that directly justiciable social and economic rights, like other rights provisions, would be given effect as a matter of interpretation. Devolved legislation could be struck down where appropriate, and statements of incompatibility could be issued in respect of primary legislation.

> **Box 15: Draft Bill of Rights: general provision to govern social and economic rights**
>
> '1. Since poverty and social exclusion represent a fundamental denial of human dignity, the protection of social and economic rights is an integral part of the delivery of effective human rights. All public bodies through which any of the legislative, executive or judicial powers of the State are exercised in Northern Ireland (in particular the Northern Ireland Executive and Northern Ireland Assembly) shall therefore take legislative and/or other measures to develop and enforce programmatic responses to the social and economic rights set out below. In doing so, all public bodies will allocate resources in a proportionate and non-discriminatory manner, as set out in the non-discrimination clause 4(4) of this Bill of Rights. All public bodies shall be required to consult and to create mechanisms which facilitate and promote the development of policies and programmes to ensure social and economic inclusion for all citizens. Legal remedies shall protect the due process and equality rights of all citizens in respect of social and economic rights.'
>
> (Northern Ireland Human Rights Commission, 2001, 'Making a Bill of Rights for Northern Ireland', www.nihrc.org)

It may be argued that Northern Ireland is subject to special circumstances which justify the enhancement of ESC rights, as the majority of the people who have suffered during the troubles have been those on low incomes or socially excluded. Yet developments in relation to ESC rights in Northern Ireland may prove influential in the growing debate on the scope and structures for human rights promotion in the rest of the UK.

The Parliamentary Joint Committee on Human Rights is presently conducting an enquiry to establish whether there is a need for a UK Human Rights Commission. In addition, the Scottish Executive has published a consultation paper on whether Scotland requires a Human Rights Commission, and what form it might take.[65] Advantage should be taken of these developments to increase the pressure for Human Rights Commissions to be set up in respect of the rest of the United Kingdom.

Implementing ESC rights across the UK

The Labour government introduced a substantial programme of constitutional reform with an emphasis on civil and political rights during its first term of office, beginning in 1997. (See Box 16.) This programme has had the effect of increasing individual rights and shifting power away from central government. Key aspects have included devolution for Scotland and Wales and Northern Ireland, and proposed legislation guaranteeing freedom of information. However, its approach to social and economic policy has not tended to be a rights-based one.

It is important, however, to consider the government's overall approach to human rights, and the opportunities which do exist for developing ESC rights in the UK. These arise primarily via the introduction of the 1998 Human Rights Act, and the development of anti-discrimination legislation.

Introduction to the 1998 Human Rights Act

At the core of the government's reform programme is the Human Rights Act 1998, which incorporates into UK law the civil and political rights (and some ESC rights) set out in the European Convention on Human Rights. Having received Royal Assent on 9 November 1998, the Act came into effect on 2 October 2000. The effect of the Human Rights Act is as follows:

- all people within the UK are guaranteed the rights set out in the European Convention on Human Rights (ECHR), which are primarily civil and political;
- individuals are able to assert these rights in the UK courts and tribunals;
- the State and other public authorities will

> **Box 16: Rights in the UK – a summary of the government's recent actions to promote human rights at the national level**[66]
>
> - Incorporation of the ECHR into UK law through the 1998 Human Rights Act.
> - Abolition of the death penalty for the last remaining civilian offences; ratification of Protocol 6 of the ECHR; and announcement of intended ratification of the Second Optional Protocol to the UN International Covenant on Civil and Political Rights (both instruments prohibiting use of the death penalty).
> - Changes in the procedures for trial of young offenders in the Crown Court; drafting of Criminal Justice and Court Service Act to give courts the power to set minimum periods of detention for young offenders, following the adverse judgement of the European Court of Human Rights in the case of the youths convicted of murdering Jamie Bulger.
> - The establishment of the Northern Ireland Human Rights Commission, a central feature of the Belfast Agreement of 10 April 1998.
> - The enactment of the Freedom of Information Act.
> - Ratification of International Labour Organisation Convention 111 on discrimination in employment, ILO Convention 138 on the minimum age for employment, and ILO Convention 182 on the elimination of the worst forms of child labour.
> - Appointment of a Minister for Women in the Cabinet, supported by the Women's Unit, to ensure that women's interests are integrated into policy formulation.
> - Implementation of the Disability Discrimination Act, intended to make services more accessible to disabled people; and the establishment of a Disability Rights Commission.
> - Race Relations (Amendment) Act, making it unlawful for any public authority, including the police, to discriminate or victimise on racial grounds in carrying out their functions.
> - The development of a National Plan to combat the commercial sexual exploitation of children.

need to ensure that their actions meet minimum human rights standards, and they can be held accountable if they do not;

- the supremacy of Parliament is retained: the courts do not have the power to strike down legislation, passed by Parliament, which is in breach of human rights, only to make a 'declaration' that it violates the rights in the HRA, and it will then be the responsibility of the government and Parliament to change the law.

The Act will help to develop a rights-related culture. It will have an effect on the courts, on Parliament, and on public administration.

Parliament

Significantly, the Act requires Ministers to certify whether legislation is compatible with Convention rights. This provision gives NGOs the opportunity to comment on the human rights implications of proposed legislation. In addition, a joint Parliamentary Committee on Human Rights has been set up with a broad remit, covering all human rights, and empowered to hold inquiries.

Courts

For the first time, the UK courts will have to develop their own human rights case law, which will draw upon and must not fall below the judgements of the European Court of Human Rights. The courts will also be able to use other international instruments, including those on ESC rights, to help them to interpret and clarify the scope of the ECHR.

Public administration

The Human Rights Act 1998 will require all those exercising public functions (such as government departments, the police, and some NGOs) to act in compliance with the ECHR. This means that they need to examine their policy and practice afresh, to ensure that human rights principles are embedded within them. The Home Office set up a Human Rights Task Force, including representatives of the government, the devolved authorities, and

NGOs, to assist in implementing the Act and educating the public about its implications. To this end, the Task Force has assisted in the production of guidance materials for public authorities and a study guide for individuals.

A significant weakness of the new Act is the failure to provide for the appointment of a Human Rights Commission to secure and promote the new human rights culture (unlike in Northern Ireland). Most NGOs argued strongly for the need for an independent Human Rights Commission to promote human rights principles and practice, by offering information and training, by conducting research and inquiries to monitor human rights compliance, and also by assisting individuals to assert their rights. For the present, the government has rejected this option; but it is being explored by the new joint Parliamentary Committee on Human Rights.

ESC rights implications of the Human Rights Act

While the ECHR focuses on civil and political rights, and its counterpart, the European Social Charter, focuses on ESC rights, in reality the demarcation lines between the two instruments are blurred. There are several areas of overlap.[67]

Although it is the ECHR (and not the European Social Charter) that is being incorporated into UK law, the fact that some of the provisions are linked means that it is essential for public authorities (including NGOs) and others interested in promoting ESC rights in the UK to explore fully the potential of the new Act. This may involve engaging in public debate over whether or not a particular provision breaches the Act; supporting individual claimants in taking challenges to the courts; and ensuring that the actions of all public organisations are compatible with ECHR rights.

In addition, there is a strong argument that some of the ECHR rights themselves are, or have developed into, protection for ESC rights. The rights to education and property (which include some social-security benefits), to marry and found a family, and to freedom of religion and belief are essentially ESC rights. The right to private life, among others, has been developed so as to include environmental protection, choice of lifestyle and dress, and sexual orientation, and can include protection against loss of home (for example, through eviction). Articles 2 and 3 have implications for health care and for some minimum level of State support for the destitute.

Examples of issues with an ESC rights dimension which are likely to be affected by the Human Rights Act are highlighted in Box 17.

Another important feature of the Human Rights Act 1998 is that UK courts will develop their own human rights jurisprudence. While domestic courts will have to take Strasbourg case law into account,[68] they will not, however, be bound by it, and other international and regional human rights standards may be cited in courts – especially in areas where ECHR case law is weak or underdeveloped. This could result in more extensive referral by UK courts to the principles set out in key instruments covering ESC rights.

Within this new legal culture, there may also be a role for NGOs to make expert submissions ('interventions') in particular cases, to assist the court by providing factual material which would otherwise not be available to it.[69] Examples of successful interventions by NGOs before the European Court of Human Rights (EctHR) and the European Court of Justice (ECJ) already exist.[70]

Legislation prohibiting discrimination

Apart from the possibilities for creative interpretation of the Human Rights Act, domestic law provides some protection of ESC rights under the umbrella of anti-discrimination provisions. While there is no statutory or constitutional right to equality in UK law, there are several statutes which attempt to address various types of discrimination.

Since the 1970s the legal framework to combat discrimination in the UK has rested upon the pillars of the Equal Pay Act 1970, the Sex Discrimination Act 1975, and the Race Relations Act 1976. The framework has been expanded more recently by the introduction of the Disability Discrimination Act 1995. However, there is no legislation relating to discrimination on the grounds of religion, sexual orientation, or age.[71]

The government has acknowledged some shortcomings in the existing legislation. Prompted in particular by the findings of the Macpherson Report into the murder of

> **Box 17: Rights under the Human Rights Act which have an ESC dimension**
>
> - *Asylum:* as a result of the Immigration and Asylum Act 1999, asylum seekers are being dispersed throughout the country and given limited financial provision, based on a voucher system. However, some of the provisions of the Human Rights Act provide a bottom line below which those support arrangements must not fall. For example, they may be challengeable under Article 8 (the right to respect for private and family life) if they result, over a significant period of time, in asylum seekers being unable to live a normal life within society and maintain relationships with their families and communities. Such circumstances will additionally be open to challenge under Article 14 (freedom from discrimination) if it can be shown that individuals are subject to discrimination in the application of the law. If support is withdrawn while an asylum claim is still live, this could raise issues under Article 3, by forcing asylum seekers either to risk returning to inhuman and degrading treatment, or to experience it in this country. Issues are also raised under Article 5 ECHR (the right to liberty) where asylum seekers are detained unnecessarily or indiscriminately.
>
> - In addition, support and accommodation may be removed or refused in certain circumstances (for example, following an unsuccessful appeal but prior to judicial review; or for those who are not considered 'destitute'). In certain circumstances, this could breach the ECHR by undermining the protection of Article 8 or even, in extreme cases, Article 3. It is also arguably contrary to Article 33 of the 1951 UN Refugee Convention.[72]
>
> - *Legal aid:* Legal aid is not available in the UK to pay for representation before tribunals where key ESC rights can be claimed. Although Article 6 does not require the provision of legal aid in respect of all civil cases, it may do so where the issues are sufficiently complex and important. For example, the absence of legal aid for a complex social security matter before the Social Security Commissioner, or in relation to a difficult sexual harassment case before an employment tribunal could raise the question of whether the access to justice in each case was 'real and effective'.[73]
>
> - *Housing repossession:* In such cases, a landlord may be required to show that a less intrusive measure (such as distraint of earnings) had been tried, or was not viable, before evicting a tenant from rented property (Article 8 and Article 1, Protocol 1).
>
> - *Social security and tax:* Laws which discriminate on the grounds of sex have been challenged in the case of *MacGregor v UK*.[74] The European Commission of Human Rights held admissible a complaint that the applicant was a victim of a violation of Article 14 (prohibition of discrimination) in conjunction with Protocol 1, Article 1 (protection of property) in relation to laws which allowed an exemption from tax for women caring for their disabled husbands, but not for men caring for disabled wives. Three similar cases involving challenges by a widower against the UK for ineligibility for widow's benefits, after being declared admissible, resulted in friendly settlements, in which the government agreed to pay sums equivalent to the benefits that the claimants would have received had they been widows, until the legislation changes.[75]
>
> - In addition, benefits where entitlement is linked to contributions are deemed to be property rights under Protocol 1, Article 1. However, social-security benefits that are based *solely* on policy considerations rather than contributions paid by the beneficiary are unlikely to be protected under Protocol 1.
>
> - *Parental 'bind-over':* Youth courts have the power – and in relation to under-16s a duty – to order the parent or guardian to enter into a recognisance to take proper care of and exercise proper control over a child convicted of a criminal offence. Refusal on the part of the parent, if considered unreasonable, may result in a fine of £1000. Under Article 7 ('no punishment without law'), and the related principle of 'legal certainty', the law is required to spell out in clear terms exactly what behaviour is permitted or prohibited. Parents may

> therefore challenge the 'bind-over' on the grounds that, when originally made, the order did not specify the exact action that they had to take to avoid forfeiture.
> - *Conditions of detention:* This is an area where Article 3 ('inhuman or degrading treatment') may well be the subject of litigation. Recent ECHR case-law suggests that the standard of poor conditions which would have to be met before a violation could be deemed to have taken place is considerable. However, ill-treatment which falls short of the Article 3 threshold may still be sufficient to amount to a breach of Article 8, if it undermines someone's human dignity in a way which is not necessary or proportional to the harm done.
> - *Education:* Article 2 of Protocol 1 (right to education) may be used in cases where disruptive children have been excluded or expelled from school, especially if inadequate resources are made available for home education or other alternatives. The same Article may also be used in combination with Article 14 (freedom from discrimination) in challenges to circumstances in which the religious and cultural needs of one ethnic minority or religious or political group are given better provision than those of another. Article 14 can also be used if exclusion or expulsion affects different groups differently without a reasonable objective justification (for instance, a school/authority would have to provide good reasons if it was shown that the majority of those excluded were African-Caribbean). In addition, Article 14 could apply if groups with different needs were treated identically without reasonable justification (for example, treating non-native speakers of English in the same way as native English speakers). However, overall this Article is relatively weak, as the burden of establishing that the State has actively denied the right to education falls on the individual.
> - *Rationing of health care:* Articles 2, 3, and 8 may also be invoked to challenge decisions where treatment is withheld; in one recent case concerning refusal by a London health trust to supply pain-relieving therapy to a woman with severe mental disabilities, the case was settled out of court.[76] There may also be implications for Article 14 where there is rationing of health care for a particular group, such as the elderly or those without a settled lifestyle.

Stephen Lawrence, the Race Relations (Amendment) Act has extended the application of the Race Relations Act 1975 to the police and public authorities, to make it unlawful for such authorities to discriminate on racial grounds in carrying out any of their functions.[77] The Act also places a positive duty on public authorities, which will give statutory force to the imperative of tackling institutional racism. Examples of the possible effects of the Act are set out in Box 18.

In addition, the powers of the Commission for Racial Equality (CRE) and the Equal Opportunities Commission (EOC) will be matched to those of the Disability Rights Commission, and barriers which prevent the equality commissions working together on common issues and joint guidance will be removed.

The introduction of the Human Rights Act 1998 is also an important development in the protection from discrimination. Article 14 of the ECHR prohibits discrimination in the enjoyment of the rights and freedoms guaranteed by the Convention. It does not provide a free-standing prohibition of discrimination: it is necessary to link the discrimination to another Convention right, although that right does not need to have been breached (for example, discriminatory detention practices, where certain groups are more likely than others to be imprisoned in the same circumstances, could breach Article 14, read with Article 5, even if the detention itself was lawful under Article 5). In addition, the grounds for discrimination under Article 14 are non-exhaustive. They include not only sex and race, but also language, religion, political or other opinion, national or social origin, property, birth or 'other status'. The category 'other status' includes sexual orientation[78] and has also permitted arguments on the basis of discrimination on the grounds of age,[79] disability, birth inside or outside marriage,[80] marital status,[81] trade union status,[82] poverty,[83] geographical location, or education. It is important to note in this context that the Council of Europe has recently opened Protocol 12 for ratification;[84] this Protocol provides a free-standing prohibition against discrimination.

> **Box 18: Examples of grounds for claims of discrimination under the Race Relations (Amendment) Act**
>
> - A black prisoner who is subjected to harsher discipline because all black prisoners are regarded as being 'more aggressive' may claim direct discrimination.
> - If a local medical practice refused to accept as patients tenants from particular housing estates which had disproportionately large numbers of ethnic-minority households, this could constitute unlawful indirect discrimination, unless the surgery could justify its action.
> - A person who is regularly stopped by the police for no legitimate reason after giving a statement in support of a friend's complaint of racism by the police may well be able to bring a case of victimisation against the police.
>
> (Commission for Racial Equality, 2000, 'The Race Relations (Amendment) Bill: questions and answers')

Once it enters into force, individuals to whom it applies will be able to challenge all discriminatory actions by public bodies, even if no other Convention rights are involved. At present, the UK government has no plans to ratify this important provision.

In Northern Ireland, a statutory equality duty has been implemented, which applies to all public bodies. This means that in future they must promote equality of opportunity regardless of political or religious opinion, sexual orientation, gender, race, age, having or not having dependants, marital status, or disability. Apart from ensuring that equality is at the heart of government, it means that policy makers are obliged to engage with those affected by the policy. The legislation lays down detailed measures which must be followed, and this involves carrying out impact assessments in respect of the various interest groups affected.

Summary

The UK government has signalled its support for the domestic protection of human rights in a number of ways, prime among which is the 1998 Human Rights Act. In general, it has emphasised the protection of civil and political rights. While recognising the indivisibility of rights when making statements in the context of its foreign policy, the government places greater emphasis upon the duties of individuals in domestic social-policy areas. However, the recent reforms in the constitutional arrangements for Northern Ireland and Scotland have shown a greater willingness on the part of the government to acknowledge the importance and place of ESC rights in the domestic realm.

ESC rights are not expressly recognised as rights under domestic law. However, issues such as housing, employment, education, benefits, and health and safety legislation are addressed in practice. And while there is no right to equality under UK law, existing legislation does provide protection from discrimination in some areas; this is likely to expand, with amendments to the Race Relations Act and the establishment of a Disability Rights Commission.

Despite the primary impact of the Human Rights Act on the protection of civil and political rights, it may now be easier to interpret some of its provisions expansively to include certain ESC rights, as the arguments about non-justiciability of these rights become weaker. Courts should be encouraged to take an expansive view of the rights they are there to protect, developing ECHR jurisprudence where possible, and using ESC rights as standards when interpreting the law.

4 The European framework for promoting and protecting ESC rights

This chapter considers the European framework[85] which can be used to promote ESC rights. The European Union is discussed first, since it is arguably the most important arena outside the UK in which to secure greater protection for ESC rights, and one where the NGO sector might wish to concentrate its efforts. Council of Europe instruments for protecting ESC rights (principally the European Social Charter) are examined thereafter.

The European Union and ESC rights

EU competence in relation to social policy is most relevant in respect of ESC rights. The stated aims of EU action in this area are the improvement of living and working conditions, the stimulation of employment and equality of opportunity, and the development of minimum social protection. However, important aspects of social and labour law remain a national responsibility.

While the EU institutions are not currently governed by a legally enforceable human rights instrument, they have been active in the promotion of economic and social rights. Measures adopted by the EU in this field, including directives which require Member States to transpose their provisions into national law, have included the following:

- provisions to combat sex discrimination;
- protection of equal pay for women and men;
- the regulation of working time;
- the rights of workers to be notified and consulted on conditions relating to contracts;
- minimum health-and-safety standards in the workplace;
- protection of workers under the age of 18;
- protection of pregnant workers;
- regulation of parental leave;
- improvement of working conditions;
- protection of disabled persons.

In the field of sex discrimination, in particular, there has been a significant development of social law and policy. Article 119 (equal pay for equal work) of the EC Treaty[86] has provided the basis for the Equal Pay Directive 1975 and a number of directives on equal treatment in the field of employment, social security, occupational pension schemes, and self-employment. No other area of social policy has so far matched this development.

The 1997 Treaty of Amsterdam amended the 1992 Maastricht Treaty so as to empower the EU as a whole to engage in a wide range of policy making on social issues, respecting the principle of subsidiarity (i.e. decisions should be taken at the lowest level possible).[87] In addition, the Treaty introduced new provisions, permitting action relating to equal opportunities, social exclusion, anti-discrimination measures, and public health. Moreover, the EU Council of Ministers[88] (the EU institution composed of the heads of Member States with the ultimate legislative power) can adopt various social measures in the following fields:

- improvement of the working environment to protect workers' health and safety;
- improving working conditions;
- informing and consulting workers;
- the integration of persons excluded from the labour market;
- equal opportunities for men and women with regard to the labour market and treatment at work.

One of the key provisions of the Treaty of Amsterdam is the anti-discrimination clause Article 13, which has given the EU legal competence for the first time to tackle discrimination on grounds other than sex: grounds such as race, religion, disability, and sexual orientation (see Box 19). Another is Article 137, which has provided the foundation for the setting of EU objectives to combat poverty and social exclusion by the Nice European Council meeting in December 2000; following on from this, Member States have had to draw up National Action Plans in line with these objectives, and will have to revise these Plans every two years.

The amendments introduced by the Treaty of Amsterdam have also enhanced the importance of human rights within the EU legal order. The Treaty affirms the EU's commitment to human rights and proclaims that the EU *'is founded on the principles of liberty, democracy, respect for human rights and fundamental freedoms and the rule of law'*.[90] It confirms attachment to 'fundamental social rights as defined in the Council of Europe European Social Charter' (see below) 'and the Community Charter of the Fundamental Social Rights of Workers'.[91]

However, the EU treaties are not human rights treaties and, while they protect some ESC entitlements, the treaty provisions and other EU instruments focus on social policy rather than on 'rights'. Also, EU law protects a limited range of social entitlements: for example, there are no treaty provisions for an adequate standard of living or housing.[92]

The 'Charter of Fundamental Rights'

The debate on a separate EU Charter of Fundamental Rights began in earnest with the 1995 report of the *Comité des Sages* on civic and social rights,[93] which recommended – among other things – the inclusion of a minimum core of fundamental rights in the EU treaties.

Building on this initial work, the new Charter was drawn up by a Convention composed by representatives of national governments, national parliaments, the European Parliament, and the Commission. It was formally and jointly adopted on 7 December 2000 by the European Council, the European Parliament, and the European Commission.[94] It has no binding force on Member States and will not impose legal obligations upon them. Article 51 states that the Charter 'does not establish any new power or task for the Community or the Union or modify powers or tasks defined by the Treaties'.

Nevertheless, the Charter marks an important milestone in the history of the European Union, underlining the support of the 15 governments for all human rights, with no distinction being drawn between ESC rights and civil and political rights. It is to be hoped that in due course a direct reference to the Charter will be inserted within Article 6 of the Treaty of the European Union, so that the protection of fundamental rights is placed at the heart of the Union's objectives.

Among the rights included in the Charter are the following, which have implications for ESC rights:

- the right to education (Article 14)
- freedom to choose an occupation and the right to engage in work (Article 15)
- the right to property (Article 17)
- equality before the law (Article 20)
- non-discrimination (Article 21)
- the right to cultural, religious, and linguistic diversity (Article 22)
- equality between men and women (Article 23)
- the rights of children (Article 24)
- the rights of older people (Article 25)

> **Box 19: The Article 13 anti-discrimination clause (EC Treaty)**
>
> Non-discrimination is a fundamental principle of EU law, but EU equal-opportunities legislation has, in the past, focused principally on gender discrimination in the field of employment. The result has been an expansive development of sex-discrimination legislation in the UK.
>
> Two directives have recently been agreed under Article 13. The first deals with discrimination on grounds of racial or ethnic origin. It covers not only the field of employment, but also 'social protection and social security, social advantages, education including grants and scholarships, access and supply of goods and services and cultural activities'.
>
> The second was agreed on 27 November 2000, and must be implemented by 2 December 2003.[89] It covers discrimination (in the field of employment only) on the grounds of racial or ethnic origin, religion or belief, disability, age, or sexual orientation. This will apply to conditions for access to employment, self-employment and occupation, including selection criteria and recruitment conditions; access to vocational guidance and training; employment and working conditions, including dismissals, pay, and membership of, involvement in, and benefits from organisations of workers or employers, and professional organisations.

- integration of people with disabilities (Article 26)
- the right of collective bargaining and action (Article 28)
- fair and just working conditions (Article 31)
- entitlement to social security and social assistance (Article 34).
- health care (Article 35)
- consumer protection (Article 38).

However, overall it is weaker than the Council of Europe's Revised Social Charter (see below) in several respects crucial to combating poverty and social exclusion, such as the right to good-quality social services, the right to a minimum income, the right to work, and the right to housing.

> **Box 20: Campaigning on the Charter of Fundamental Rights at EU level**
>
> 'The Platform of European Social NGOs and the ETUC (European Trade Union Confederation) waged an effective campaign on the Charter in 2000, releasing a joint campaign paper. They have now agreed to further work on the implementation and improvement of the Charter and have resolved to increase co-operation in combating social exclusion and promoting social protection. In addition they have decided to work together to ensure that organised civil society plays an important role in EU policy-making.'
>
> (Platform/ETUC Campaign Paper, www.socialplatform.org)

NGO activities in the EU context

At present NGOs have limited input into the policy-making procedures of the EU, and they do not play an active role in responding to policy or other documents. This is due partly to the lack of awareness of EU law and policy making among NGOs, and partly to the obscure nature of EU decision-making processes and the practical difficulties in lobbying a Brussels-based bureaucracy from abroad.

However, there is much potential for NGOs to increase their role in EU affairs. The Treaty of Amsterdam allows national parliaments to scrutinise EU directives in draft. In the UK this is undertaken by Parliamentary Committees in both the Houses of Parliament, which invite evidence from interested groups and individuals (see below). NGOs may also lobby at EU level for changes to European policies, and they may use EU law to campaign for changes to national legislation. Below we set out some of the options available to NGOs.

Influencing European policies

There are several ways in which NGOs can influence EU legislation and policy making at both the domestic and European levels. At the domestic level, NGOs seeking to promote a particular issue can lobby the Minister with responsibility for that issue. The power of the Parliamentary scrutiny committees[95] considering draft EU directives to receive written and oral evidence provides an excellent opportunity for NGOs to exert influence. Thus, where the EU has drafted a directive on a matter of social policy, NGOs may lobby the Minister responsible, the House of Commons Scrutiny Select Committee, or the House of Lords European Union Committee.

At the level of the EU, NGOs may lobby the European Commission (in effect, the EU's civil service – see glossary) to introduce a proposal for a directive to give effect to a particular right. A good example is provided by

> **Box 21: NGO advocacy in relation to House of Lords scrutiny of EU policy-making**
>
> From January to March 2000, the Social Affairs, Education, and Home Affairs Sub-Committee of the House of Lords European Union Committee took written and oral evidence from a number of organisations on the EU draft directives under Article 13 of the Treaty of Amsterdam, including JUSTICE, Liberty, the Commission for Racial Equality, the Trades Union Congress, the Confederation of British Industry, Age Concern, and the Equal Opportunities Commission. As a result of further lobbying of MEPs, JUSTICE was successful in securing agreement to an amendment to the Race Directive on the definition of indirect discrimination (which was also carried over into the EU Framework Directive).

Article 13 of the EC Treaty, which provides that the EU may adopt legislative measures to combat discrimination. This gives scope for NGOs to draft proposals for such legislation and to lobby the Commission to adopt them. The achievements of the Starting Line Group provide a good example: following the adoption of Article 13, for which it had lobbied, the Group drafted a proposal for secondary legislation to give effect to this Article (see Box 22).

A further possibility for NGO action at the EU level is lobbying for amendments to EU treaties. Indeed, NGOs may also lobby national governments and European institutions such as the European Commission[96] or the European Parliament[97] for this purpose. Since the 1980s, the EC Treaty has been regularly updated by amending treaties, such as the Maastricht Treaty and the Treaty of Amsterdam. These treaties are the result of 'Intergovernmental Conferences', which are standing conferences (for up to two years) involving representatives from each of the Member States.

The next opportunity to campaign for amendments to the founding treaties of the European Union will be during the Intergovernmental Conference 2004. An intergovernmental conference is an ideal opportunity for an NGO to promote its agenda.

Influencing interpretation of EU law: litigation

For EU citizens the European Court of Justice has proved to be an influential court, which has developed a dynamic body of case law. For example, in the case of *P v S and Cornwall County Council*,[98] the ECJ decided that the Equal Treatment Directive covered cases of gender reassignment, and thus extended the concept of sex equality.

Litigation before the ECJ is an option for influencing the interpretation of EU law but, until the rules on standing are improved, it remains a limited one. Review by the ECJ falls into two types of case: preliminary rulings (Article 234 of the EC Treaty) and direct actions (Article 230).

National courts carry out primary supervision of EU law. Thus where a female employee complains of sex discrimination, a matter covered by the EU Equal Treatment Directive, litigation is pursued, in the first instance, in a domestic employment tribunal. EU law may be relied upon in the employment tribunal, or any other tribunal or court which may be called upon to adjudicate in the case. Where a novel or particularly complex point of law arises in a case, the national court or tribunal may refer these questions to the European Court of Justice for a preliminary ruling. Under this procedure the ECJ does not make any decision on the dispute itself, but interprets EU law so as to enable the national court to reach a decision. The case is then returned to the national court for a final decision. The decisions of the ECJ are binding on all courts and tribunals in Member States. ECJ decisions may have the effect of over-riding national legislation or over-ruling national court judgements if they are considered incompatible with EU law.

Direct action may be brought by Member States, EU institutions, and private applicants (individuals or organisations). However, one of the significant weaknesses of the ECJ is the restricted access for individual and group complaints. At present a complaint must relate to a 'decision' of 'direct and individual concern' to the complainant.[99] This prevents individuals and NGOs from challenging acts which infringe individual freedoms or Treaty rights when they themselves are not directly affected.

Third-party interventions in respect of litigation before the ECJ are difficult, but are possible and might usefully be considered by NGOs with legal expertise. However, the Court will permit such interventions only in limited circumstances, and few NGOs have been granted permission. An intervenor in a case must show a sufficient interest in the result of the case.[100] Furthermore, the intervenor may only

---

Box 22: The Starting Line Group and protection from racial discrimination

The experience of the Starting Line Group is a good example of the influence that an NGO can exercise at the European level. The Starting Line Group is an informal network of groups whose principal aim is to promote legal measures to combat racism and xenophobia in Europe. The Group was successful in campaigning for an amendment to the EC Treaty to provide protection from racial discrimination. It has also proposed secondary legislation, including a directive to prevent discrim-ination on the basis of race or religion, and a regulation to protect the rights of third-country nationals who are resident in the European Union.

support, or advocate the rejection of, the case already made by one of the parties.[101] Therefore, it may not be open to an intervenor to introduce all the material that she or he might deem relevant to the argument. NGOs should also be aware that an application to intervene may result in their being made a full party to the case, which may have cost implications. In respect of cases referred by the national courts for adjudication, intervention by third parties is governed by national rules.[102]

However, there is still a role for NGOs to play in providing information and advice to potential applicants, especially where there is ambiguity in EU law or confusion over implementation in national law. There may be more scope for relying on EU law in cases brought before national courts. For instance, an NGO may argue that national practices breach a fundamental rule of EU law, or that a Directive has not been implemented correctly in national law.

The Council of Europe

The Council of Europe, established in 1949, is based in Strasbourg. Its main role is to strengthen democracy, human rights, and the rule of law throughout its Member States. It is perhaps best known for the European Convention on Human Rights and the European Court of Human Rights.[103] As mentioned earlier, the ECHR offers protection mainly to civil and political rights. Its Court is empowered to entertain complaints from individuals within the jurisdiction of a State Party claiming to be victims of violations of the Convention. The Court has been in existence for some 50 years, and has generated a huge and significant body of case law. The ECHR does provide some protection for some rights traditionally regarded as ESC rights. They include:

- the prohibition against discrimination (only in relation to the exercise of another right under the Convention) – Article 14;
- the right to education – Article 2, Protocol 1;
- the right to respect for property (Article 1, Protocol 1);
- the right to respect for the home (Article 8).

In addition, some of the rights traditionally characterised as civil or political have been given broad interpretations, thereby encompassing ESC rights. NGOs have a worthwhile role to play in making interventions in relevant cases. Such interventions may be made by NGOs which can show an interest in the issue under litigation. While the complaints mechanism provided by the ECHR is highly regarded world-wide and has spawned case law which has far-reaching ramifications, the main focus is on civil and political rights. The main reason for this is the existence of another Council of Europe treaty which is far less well known, but growing in importance, namely the European Social Charter. The remaining part of this chapter will be devoted to a consideration of this instrument. It is not proposed to examine the ECHR in any detail.

The European Social Charter

The European Social Charter (the Social Charter) protects fundamental social and economic rights. The Social Charter and its 1988 Additional Protocol guarantee a series of rights in three areas: in the work environment; special protection outside of work for vulnerable groups; and universal social protection for the whole population, whether in or out of work. Parties are obliged to pursue by all appropriate means the attainment of conditions in which these rights may be effectively realised.

UK ratification of the European Social Charter

As well as adding new rights, the Revised Social Charter 1996 consolidates into one text the rights contained in the European Social Charter 1961 and the 1988 Additional Protocol. The UK government has ratified the 1961 Charter and has signed – but not ratified – the Revised Social Charter. The government has neither ratified nor signed the 1988 Additional Protocol. However, in its Annual Report 2000, the Foreign and Commonwealth Office indicated that the government would ratify the Revised Social Charter 'in due course'.[104]

Supervision of the European Social Charter

Contracting Parties are required to submit regular reports on their implementation of the Charter. The following bodies are involved in a three-stage monitoring procedure: the European Committee of Social Rights, the Governmental Committee, and the Committee of Ministers. NGOs may send comments on a government's compliance to the first two of

Box 23: The European Social Charter (1961)

- The right to work (Article 1)
- The right to just conditions of work (Article 2)
- The right to safe working conditions (Article 3)
- The right to fair remuneration, including the right of women and men to equal pay for work of equal value (Article 4)
- The right of workers to organise, and to bargain collectively (Articles 5 and 6)
- The right of children and young people to protection (Article 7)
- The right of employed women to protection (Article 8)
- The right to vocational guidance and training (Articles 9 and 10)
- The right to work in the territory of other Contracting Parties (Article 18)

Special protection outside of work for vulnerable groups

- The right of disabled people to vocational training, rehabilitation, and social resettlement (Article 15)
- The right of the family to social, legal, and economic protection (Article 16)
- The right of mothers and children to social and economic protection (Article 17)
- The right of migrant workers and their families to protection and assistance (Article 19)

Universal social protection for the whole population

- The right to protection of health (Article 11)
- The right to social security and to social and medical assistance (Articles 12 and 13)
- The right to benefit from social-welfare services (Article 14)

Contracting Parties may choose which provisions to accept when ratifying the Charter, with certain requirements as to the minimum number.

The Additional Protocol (1988)

The Additional Protocol added a further four rights to the original Charter:

- The right to equal opportunities and treatment in employment and occupational matters without discrimination on the grounds of sex (Additional Protocol, Article 1)
- The right of workers to information and consultation (Additional Protocol, Article 2)
- The right of workers to take part in the determination and improvement of working conditions (Additional Protocol, Article 3)
- The right of elderly people to social protection (Additional Protocol, Article 4)

The Revised Social Charter (1996) (entered into force 1 July 1999)

The Revised Social Charter covers 31 fundamental rights. It includes an over-arching provision protecting against discrimination in securing these rights:

- The right to protection against poverty and social exclusion (Article 30)
- The right to decent housing (Article 31)
- The right to protection in case of termination of employment (Article 24)
- The right to protection against sexual harassment and victimisation (Article 26)
- The right of workers with family responsibilities to equal opportunities and equal treatment (Article 27)
- The right of workers' representatives to protection (Article 28)
- The right of workers to be informed and consulted in collective redundancy procedures (Article 29)
- The right of workers to be informed and consulted in the event of insolvency of the employer (Article 25)

these bodies, although the second is restricted to receiving information from NGOs with consultative status with the Council of Europe.

Complaints

An Additional Protocol (1995), providing for a system for collective complaints alleging unsatisfactory application of the Charter, entered into force on 1 July 1998 for those Contracting Parties that have ratified it. They are Belgium, Cyprus, Finland, France, Greece, Ireland, Italy, Norway, Portugal, and Sweden. The UK government has neither ratified nor signed the Collective Complaints Protocol.[105]

UK compliance with the Social Charter

In its Conclusions relating to national reports for 1997-98 covering core provisions of the Charter (Articles 1, 5, 6, 12, 13, 16, and 19),[106] the European Committee of Social Rights took note of the UK government's figures for falling unemployment rates, the provision of free employment services for job-seekers; the provision of vocational training and guidance; and the maintenance of a social-security system. However, despite these positive aspects, the Committee considered that ten UK provisions were in breach of the Social Charter. Of particular concern was the narrow scope for lawful industrial action, and the possibility for an employer to dismiss all workers who have taken part in industrial action. This has been held to be a breach of Article 6(4) of the Social Charter and has been the subject of two recommendations issued to the UK government by the Committee of Ministers.[107] The Committee also found other breaches, including the following:

- excessive limitations on the right of trade unions to use their property freely; to exclude or expel individuals; and to discipline their members (Article 5);
- the possibility for employers to take measures such as increasing wage rates for employees who agree to give up their trade-union activities and collective bargaining (Article 5);
- failure to guarantee equality of treatment regarding entitlement to family allowances (Article 16);
- failure to guarantee the right of migrant workers and their families to protection and assistance (Article 19).

Box 24: Complaint of the International Commission of Jurists vs. Portugal, no. 1/1998

In response to the first-ever complaint registered under the Additional Protocol, the Committee of Social Rights considered that the situation in Portugal was not in conformity with Article 7, paragraph 1 of the Charter (prohibition of employment for children under fifteen years of age).

By 2001, ten complaints had been submitted to the Committee, covering issues such as the right to organise and to bargain collectively, prohibition against all forms of discrimination in access to employment, and the right to vocational training.

In its most recent conclusions relating to national reports for 1995-98, covering Articles 7, 8, 11, 14, 17, and 18,[108] which were examined between June and December 2000, the European Committee of Social Rights considered that the UK was not in compliance with the Charter in relation to four provisions, summarised as follows.

- The two-week mandatory rest period during summer holidays for working children still subject to compulsory education is insufficient to let children rest in order to benefit from school after the holiday (Article 7, para 3).
- As the government has not shown that the wages of all young workers have reached a level which can be considered fair, the Committee has held that the wages of adult workers breach Article 4 para. 1.
- There is no compulsory period of six weeks' post-natal leave, and statutory maternity pay is paid at an appropriate rate (90 per cent of previous earnings) for only six weeks (Article 8, para 1).
- The conditions for the employment of nationals of Contracting Parties to the Charter that are not members of the EU are excessive (Article 18, para 3).

Summary

As a result of the perceived complexity of the EU's structures and processes, some NGOs have shown themselves reluctant to engage with them.

However, the EU's competence in the field of ESC rights is relatively clear, and the opportunities for NGOs to influence EU policy and law making are numerous. Now that national parliaments have been given powers to scrutinise draft EU directives, new opportunities for NGO activity have opened up at the domestic level. NGO input is welcomed at the EU level too, and the experience of organisations and networks such as the Starting Line Group should be built upon and expanded. Given the increasing influence of the EU, and the fears, real or imagined, of its encroachment on the rights of citizens of the EU, it is crucial that NGOs engage with the EU in the field of ESC rights.

In relation to the Council of Europe Social Charter, although the UK government has so far failed to ratify the 1995 Additional Protocol providing for a system of collective complaints, there is plenty of scope for NGO activity in relation to the Charter. Indeed, NGOs might start by lobbying the government to ensure ratification of the Additional Protocol, and the setting of a timetable for ratification of the Revised Social Charter. The Conclusions of the European Committee of Social Rights provide a useful starting point from which to lobby for improvements to domestic law. In addition, NGOs might consider making submissions on elements of the UK periodic reports to the European Committee of Social Rights and the Governmental Committee.

Box 25: NGO action under the Social Charter

The Belfast-based Committee on the Administration of Justice (CAJ) considered the UK government's nineteenth report and raised several issues with the Committee. These included the following:

- that government policy on targets to reduce unemployment differentials in Britain focus on ethnic minorities but not on different communities within Northern Ireland;
- that no reference is made to the new statutory duty on public authorities in Northern Ireland to promote equality of opportunity regardless of age;
- that there are poor child-care provisions in Northern Ireland;
- that obligations to ensure fairness at work do not apply in Northern Ireland.

By raising specific points such as those listed above, the CAJ has alerted the Committee to areas requiring further questioning of the government's report. More recently, CAJ published a report on social rights in Northern Ireland, which drew extensively upon the framework of the European Social Charter.[109]

5 The international framework for promoting and protecting ESC rights

The United Nations

A large number of UN instruments address economic, social, and cultural rights. The following, examined in this chapter, are the most important:

- Universal Declaration of Human Rights (UDHR)
- International Covenant on Economic, Social and Cultural Rights (ICESCR)
- Convention on the Elimination of Discrimination Against Women (CEDAW)
- Convention on the Elimination of all forms of Racial Discrimination (CERD)
- Convention on the Rights of the Child (CRC)
- Conventions of the International Labour Organisation (ILO).[110]

Each instrument provides for a wide range of ESC rights. Some are universal in their application, while others focus on the rights of particular groups who require specific protection, such as women, ethnic minorities, children, or workers.

Aside from the UDHR, which is not a treaty, the UK government has ratified all the human rights treaties listed, and some of the ILO Conventions. The government is therefore under a duty to adhere to the provisions of each treaty. This does not mean that they have direct effect in domestic law: individuals cannot bring a complaint in domestic courts for breach of a provision. However, where domestic legislation or policy is weak or deficient, they provide guiding principles and standards for government action, and a measure by which NGOs can hold government accountable. This in turn results in the promotion of ESC rights at a national level.

Additionally, these instruments may be relied upon by the courts as aids to the interpretation of ambiguous legislation or the development of the common law. This practice is likely to increase, following the implementation of the Human Rights Act 1998, as they are recognised as additional sources of law for the interpretation of the European Convention on Human Rights. They may also be used as a guide to the formulation and implementation of public policy by government, other public authorities, and NGOs. This is particularly important for ESC rights, where litigation in the courts may not be appropriate or effective under the Human Rights Act.

The UK government and international human rights instruments

In March 1999, the government completed a review of the UK's position under international human rights treaties. While it announced its intention to undertake several positive changes with regard to civil and political rights, it was less forthcoming in relation to ESC rights.

Some improvements have been announced or implemented, for example, the intended withdrawal of a reservation to the CRC relating to the employment of 16-18 year-olds, and the ratification of ILO Convention 111 on the Elimination of Discrimination in Employment. A commitment was also made to consider ratification of the Fourth Protocol to the European Convention on Human Rights (ECHR), which includes such essential rights as the prohibition of imprisonment for debt. But further delay was signalled on the ratification of other core human rights standards (such as the rights of petition under several Conventions, including CERD).

Supervision of periodic reports by UN treaty-bodies

While each of the human rights treaties examined in this section has its own Committee with its own rules of procedure, they all have in common the State obligation to submit periodic reports on progress made towards implementation of the respective treaties. It is accordingly appropriate to make general points here about the process of examining periodic reports under the ICESCR, the CEDAW, the CERD, and the CRC.[111]

NGO participation in the supervisory process is regarded as crucial by the Committees, and is important in exposing weaknesses in a State's implementation of the treaties. Written submissions by NGOs enable the Committees to pose informed questions to State representatives on matters which a State might have presented inaccurately or in a highly partial manner. At the conclusion of the examination of a particular report, the Committees draw up Concluding Observations, which provide detailed assessment of a State's compliance, as well as suggestions and recommendations for action. Carefully documented NGO input can influence a Committee's assessment. While the Committees' Concluding Observations are not binding on States parties, they are required to be publicised widely in the State concerned. A State's compliance with a Committee's suggestions and recommendations is followed up when that Committee considers its next periodic report. Accordingly, NGOs can take advantage of the opportunities which publicity provides.

Some of the Committees which monitor compliance with the treaties examined below operate complaints mechanisms. The UK has not accepted the jurisdiction of any of the Committees to examine individual or group complaints. This is a matter which NGOs might usefully take up with the government.

> **Box 26: ESC rights contained in the Universal Declaration of Human Rights**
>
> The UDHR contains the following ESC provisions.
>
> - The right to social security and the economic, social, and cultural rights indispensable for dignity and the free development of personality (Article 22).
> - The right to work, to free choice of employment, to just and favourable conditions of work, to protection against unemployment, to equal pay for equal work, to just and favourable remuneration, and to form and join trade unions (Article 23).
> - The right to rest and leisure (Article 24).
> - The right to an adequate standard of living and to special care and assistance during motherhood and childhood (Article 25).
> - The right to education (Article 26).
> - The right freely to participate in the cultural life of the community, to enjoy the arts and share in scientific advancements (Article 27).

The Universal Declaration of Human Rights (1948)

The Universal Declaration of Human Rights (UDHR) sets common standards to facilitate the achievement of human rights and to promote their universal and effective recognition. As noted earlier, the Declaration makes no distinction between ESC rights and civil and political rights.

The UDHR was adopted as a simple resolution of the General Assembly of the United Nations. Governments do not ratify declarations. However, the UK government recognises the central importance of the UDHR and voted in favour of its adoption. The government's Annual Report on Human Rights, published in 1999, stated that 'Respect for and commitment to the human rights and fundamental freedoms set out in the Universal Declaration of Human Rights is a constant theme throughout the work of this Government'.[112]

The declaration, though not technically binding, has acquired legal force over the past 50 years, and as a result it can be usefully relied upon as a yardstick by which to measure government action or inaction. NGOs may therefore cite its provisions, as well as those of relevant treaties, in all their lobbying for and promotion of ESC rights.

International Covenant on Economic, Social and Cultural Rights (1966)

The International Covenant on Economic, Social and Cultural Rights (ICESCR) is the major UN treaty protecting ESC rights. It complements the International Covenant on Civil and Political Rights (ICCPR).

The UK ratified the ICESCR on 20 May 1976, and the treaty entered into force in respect of the UK on 20 August 1976.

Supervision of the ICESCR is limited to examination of States' periodic reports by the Committee on Economic Social and Cultural Rights. Besides receiving written submissions

> **Box 27: Rights contained in the ICESCR**
>
> Economic rights, covered in Articles 6–9, include the following:
>
> - the right to earn a living and to choose a job (Article 6);
> - the right to just and favourable conditions of work, including the right to fair and equal remuneration, safe and healthy working conditions, equal opportunity for promotion, and opportunities for rest, leisure and paid holidays (Article 7);
> - the right to form and join trade unions, the right of trade unions to function freely, and the right to strike (Article 8);
> - the right to social security, including social insurance (Article 9).
>
> Social rights, covered in Articles 10–13, include the following:
>
> - the right to family protection and assistance, including special protection for mothers before and after childbirth, and the protection of children and young persons from economic and social exploitation (Article 10);
> - the right of everyone to an adequate standard of living for himself and his family, including adequate food, clothing, and housing, and the continuous improvement of living conditions (Article 11);
> - the right to the highest attainable standard of physical and mental health (Article 12);
> - the right to education, including free and compulsory primary education (Article 13). Countries which, at the time of ratification, do not have a system of compulsory primary education must work out and adopt a detailed plan for its progressive implementation (Article 14).
>
> Cultural rights and the right to enjoy the benefits of scientific progress are covered in Article 15.

from NGOs, the Committee permits oral representations to be made by NGOs (see Box 28). These may be made to the pre-sessional working group for the Committee and to the Committee session itself.

The ICESCR differs from the International Covenant on Civil and Political Rights (ICCPR) and other treaties protecting civil and political rights in that it contains the notion of *progressive realisation of rights*. This term was interpreted by some States as giving them licence to postpone many of their obligations under the treaty indefinitely. As a result, the Limburg Principles and the Maastricht Guidelines were drafted by groups of experts, as aids to the interpretation of this and other provisions of the Covenant.[113]

As already mentioned, there is, as yet, no mechanism by which individuals or groups can make formal communications concerning alleged violations of the rights recognised in the ICESCR. However, in 2001 the Commission on Human Rights appointed an independent expert to examine the question of a draft Optional Protocol.[114] The Protocol would provide a complaints mechanism for individuals in those States which ratify it. It is also proposed that the right to submit a complaint should extend to individuals and groups who act on behalf of alleged victims. This would give NGOs an additional means to highlight concerns and to influence government policy.

UK compliance with ICESCR

The UN Committee on Economic Social and Cultural Rights (CESCR) recognises that there exists in the UK an extensive and elaborate administrative infrastructure which gives effect to socio-economic rights.[115] In their most recent Conclusions on the UK government's periodic reports, the CESCR has noted official figures on declining unemployment rates; the provision of free employment services for job-seekers; the provision of vocational training and guidance; and the maintenance of a social-security system. In addition, the CESCR has welcomed government initiatives such as the 'Welfare to Work' and 'New Deal' schemes, the incorporation of the European Convention on Human Rights, the introduction of a national minimum wage, and the establishment of a Disability Rights Commission.[116]

Despite these developments, the Committee found that with regard to economic rights, and trade union rights in particular, the UK government was in breach of the ICESCR. Concern was also expressed over the failure to give adequate protection to a number of social rights. UK labour laws have been repeatedly criticised by the Committee. The CESCR has held that the failure to incorporate the right to strike into national law constitutes a breach of Article 8 of the ICESCR:

The Committee considers that the common law approach recognising only the freedom to strike, and the concept that strike action constitutes a fundamental breach of contract justifying dismissal, is not consistent with protection of the right to strike.[117]

The law and practice of the UK with respect to other ESC rights has been the subject of further criticism by the ICESCR. Among the principal subjects of concern were the following:

- the unacceptable levels of poverty among certain segments of the population, particularly within Northern Ireland, despite the developed state of the British economy and the progress made to reduce unemployment generally;
- the uneven distribution of economic benefits of recent gains in prosperity, resulting in a significant widening of the gap between rich and poor;
- the fact that approximately one million people do not apply for the benefits to which they are entitled;
- the high levels of discrimination against women and ethnic minorities, which result in lower pay and higher unemployment among these groups;
- the lengthy waiting periods for surgery;
- the high level of homelessness;
- the disproportionate numbers of African-Caribbean pupils who are excluded from school;
- the non-availability of legal aid for tribunals.

This is perhaps the most significant treaty dealing with ESC rights. Together with the interpretative texts mentioned, the ICESCR and its General Comments can be relied upon as authoritative sources for the interpretation of ESC entitlements in domestic cases.

Box 28: NGO action under ICESCR

In October 1997 a coalition of British NGOs, co-ordinated by Oxfam and JUSTICE, lodged a joint submission in response to the UK government's periodic report.[118] Among the key concerns were the following:

- that the UK had become one of the poorer EU countries, ranking 11th out of 15;
- that more than one in three children were living in poverty, compared with one in ten in 1980;
- that the divide between the wages of the highest and lowest paid was greater than at any time since 1986.

The coalition gave an oral presentation to the Committee, which considered the submission in its deliberations. The submission was widely reported in the media, enabling NGOs to highlight current policy concerns in social-welfare provision and to draw attention to the international legal framework.

Convention on the Elimination of all Forms of Discrimination Against Women (1979)

The Convention on the Elimination of all Forms of Discrimination against Women (CEDAW) is a UN treaty which requires States Parties to abolish sex discrimination and to promote the equality of women with men in all aspects of political, social, economic, and cultural life.

The UK has ratified CEDAW, with effect from 7 May 1986. The government has entered several reservations, affecting – among other things – its application of Article 10(c) (the elimination of stereotyped roles of men and women in all forms and at all levels of education) and Article 11 (pensions and benefits). In March 1999, the government's review of its international human rights obligations endorsed the retention of the existing UK reservations, but suggested that some of these should only be retained 'for the time being'.

In addition to the obligation to examine States' periodic reports, CEDAW is empowered to examine complaints. On 12 March 1999,[119]

> **Box 29: CEDAW provisions specifically related to the achievement of social, economic, and cultural rights**
>
> - Temporary special measures are permitted as a means of accelerating equality between men and women, and of protecting maternity (Article 4).
> - All appropriate measures should be taken to modify the social and cultural patterns of conduct of men and women, to eliminate prejudices based on the superiority of one sex above the other, and to promote recognition of the important function of child-bearing and child-rearing (Article 5).
> - All appropriate measures should be taken to ensure the equal rights of men and women in relation to education (Article 10).
> - All appropriate measures should be taken to eliminate discrimination against women in the field of employment, and in particular to protect the rights to work, to the same employment opportunities, to free choice of profession and employment, to equal pay for work of equal value, to social security, and to safe conditions of work. In addition, all appropriate measures must be taken to prevent discrimination against women on the grounds of pregnancy or maternity leave, and to ensure their effective right to work (Article 11).
> - All appropriate measures must be taken to eliminate discrimination against women in relation to health care, and to ensure equal access to health-care services, including family planning (Article 12).
> - All appropriate measures must be taken to eliminate discrimination against women in relation to other areas of economic and social life and to ensure the same rights, in particular the right to family benefits, bank loans, mortgages and other forms of financial credit and to participate in recreational activities, sports, and all aspects of cultural life (Article 13).

an Optional Complaints Protocol was adopted. It contains two procedures:

- a communications procedure allowing individual women, or groups of women, to submit claims of violations of their rights to the Committee supervising CEDAW;
- an inquiry procedure enabling the Committee to act on reliable information submitted to it, and to initiate inquiries into situations of grave or systematic violations of women's rights.

In either case, the respondent State must be a party to the Protocol.

The Optional Protocol was adopted by the General Assembly in 1999 and entered into force on 22 December 2000. By September 2001, 68 States had signed the Protocol and 27 countries had ratified it. The United Kingdom has so far neither signed nor ratified it.

UK compliance with CEDAW

In its most recent Concluding Observations,[120] the UN Committee on the Elimination of All Forms of Discrimination Against Women, reviewing the situation in the UK, welcomed the amendment of the Sex Discrimination Act (1975), the introduction of the National Minimum Wage Act 1999, and the enactment of the Human Rights Act 1998, but identified the following problems.

- The Human Rights Act does not provide for the full range of women's rights incorporated in CEDAW. In particular, Article 4(1), on measures aimed at accelerating equality (i.e. positive action), was noted as being absent from UK legislation.
- Women continue to earn less than men for similar work. In particular, women working in higher education receive lower pay and do not advance in their careers as rapidly or in the same numbers as men in this field.
- The rate of teenage conception is the highest among Western Europe. The consequences for young women are lower educational achievement, higher levels of poverty, and greater reliance on social welfare.
- Demographic changes have negative implications for older women in terms of their health, their accommodation, their incomes, and especially their pension entitlements. The committee noted the growing problem

> Box 30: NGO action under CEDAW

The Women's National Commission, which is the UK government's independent advisory group on women, includes representatives from leading NGOs such as the Fawcett Society, Gingerbread, and the Mothers' Union. The Commission, commenting on the UK government's Fourth Periodic Report to the CEDAW Committee, raised the following concerns: disparity in pay; the need to redesign work and welfare provisions to reflect the realities of women's lives; violence against women; the need to strengthen institutional mechanisms for women; and the low number of women in public and political life.

of the abuse of older people, and identified an inter-generational cycle of poverty.

International Convention on the Elimination of all Forms of Racial Discrimination (1966)

The International Convention on the Elimination of All Forms of Racial Discrimination (CERD) is a UN treaty which prohibits and condemns

... any distinction, exclusion, restriction or preference based on race, colour, descent, or national or ethnic origin which has the purpose or effect of nullifying the recognition, enjoyment or exercise, on an equal footing, of human rights and fundamental freedoms in the political, economic, social, cultural or any other field of public life (Article 1(1)).

The UK ratified CERD on 7 March 1969, and the treaty entered into force on 6 April 1969. The UK does not have any reservations and declarations which affect its application of the provisions on social, economic, and cultural rights.

Like all the other UN treaties covered in this section, the supervisory Committee for CERD welcomes written submissions from NGOs. In addition to the requirement to examine periodic reports, CERD has a complaints mechanism. Under Article 14 of CERD, claims against a State Party by an individual or group claiming to be a victim of a violation of one or more of the rights contained in CERD may be made to the Committee on a confidential basis. States Parties to CERD can decide whether or not to accept this complaints mechanism; to date the UK government has not done so.

> Box 31: CERD provisions specifically related to the achievement of ESC rights
>
> - The obligation on States Parties to take special and concrete measures to ensure the adequate development and protection of certain racial groups, or individuals belonging to them, for the purpose of guaranteeing them the full and equal enjoyment of human rights and fundamental freedoms (Article 2(2)).
>
> - The rights of everyone, without distinction as to race, colour, or national or ethnic origin, to equality before the law in relation to ESC rights, in particular the right to work, to free choice of employment, to just and favourable conditions of work, to equal pay for equal work, to just and favourable remuneration, to form and join trade unions, to housing, to public health, medical care, social security and social services, to education and training, and to equal participation in cultural activities (Article 5(e)).

UK compliance with CERD

The most recent conclusions of the CERD Committee on the UK[121] welcomed a number of government initiatives, including the following: the establishment by the Home Secretary of the Race Relations Forum; the setting up of a Ministerial Social Exclusion Unit to rehabilitate inner-city areas where a high proportion of national and ethnic minorities live; and the launching of the New Deal Scheme, which includes a pro-active strategy to introduce young members of national and ethnic minorities to the labour market. It also welcomed initiatives taken to promote the socio-economic situation of Roma travellers.

On ESC rights, the Committee expressed concern over the position of asylum seekers in the UK, particularly the dispersal system, which, it stated, may hamper their access to necessary services, including health care and

> **Box 32: NGO action under CERD**
>
> In 2000, a group of 28 organisations, including Liberty, the 1990 Trust, the Refugee Council, and the Joint Council for the Welfare of Immigrants, worked together to prepare a joint NGO submission for the Committee. The submission challenged the government's report, arguing (for example) that people from ethnic minorities are not sufficiently protected in the UK, and that government legislation in relation to asylum has fuelled racial tension. A small delegation of representatives attended the Committee meeting, and an opportunity was provided for them to give a present-ation to Committee members regarding concerns and issues. This was the second time that UK organisations had made such a submission to CERD. The conclusions of the Committee reflected the views of the non-government organisations.

education, as well as legal advice. It also expressed concern over the high level of unemployment among ethnic-minority groups, the existence of racial harassment and bullying in schools, and the fact that ethnic minorities continue to be disproportionately excluded from schools.

The Convention on the Rights of the Child (1989)

The Convention on the Rights of the Child (CRC) has been ratified more widely and quickly than any other international human rights instrument. It is especially significant in that it combines the whole family of rights – not only civil and political entitlements, but also economic, social, and cultural rights – in one instrument.

The UK ratified the CRC on 16 December 1991, with effect from 15 January 1992. The UK has made certain reservations to the CRC: for example, it has reserved the right to accommodate young offenders with adults where it deems necessary, and to apply any provision of UK domestic immigration legislation and practice without reference to the Convention. However, following the government's review of its international human rights obligations in March 1999 and the implementation of the EU Young Workers Directive, the government is withdrawing its reservation, which governs the right of the child to be protected from economic exploitation and hazardous or harmful work.

The CRC is supervised only by means of periodic reports. Despite the fact that there is no complaints procedure, the wide ratification and moral authority of the CRC has greatly increased the pressure on governments to promote and protect children's rights.

UK compliance with the CRC

The Committee on the Rights of the Child, in its Concluding Observations[122] on the UK's first periodic report (1995), was highly critical and identified the following problems.

- The UK reservation relating to national immigration policy and practice was not compatible with the principles and provisions of the Convention.

- Insufficient consideration had been given to the establishment of mechanisms to co-ordinate and monitor the implementation of the rights of the child.

- Insufficient expenditure was allocated to the social sector, both within the UK and within the context of its policy on international development.

- The principle of acting in the best interests of the child was not reflected in legislation on matters such as health care, education, and social security.

- The health status of children of certain socio-economic groups and those belonging to ethnic minorities gave rise to concern.

- Increasing numbers of children were living in poverty, and there was particular concern that changes in the regulations relating to benefit entitlements for young people might have contributed to the increase in the number of young homeless people.

- The situation of Gypsy and Traveller children was a matter of concern, especially with regard to their access to basic services and the provision of caravan sites.

> **Box 33: Rights guaranteed by the Convention on the Rights of the Child (CRC)**
>
> All the rights contained in the CRC are subject to the following four general principles:
>
> - the right to non-discrimination (Article 2(1));
> - the principle that, in all actions concerning children taken by public authorities, the best interests of the child shall be a primary consideration (Article 3(1));
> - the right of every child to life, survival, and development (Article 6);
> - the right of children to have their views given due weight, in accordance with their age and maturity (Article 12).
>
> Article 4 makes it clear that States parties are under an obligation to take measures to achieve the realisation of these rights 'to the maximum extent of their available resources'. The CRC contains the following provisions which specifically relate to the achievement of social, economic, and cultural rights:
>
> - the right of every child to enjoy the highest attainable standard of health and the facilities for the treatment of illness and rehabilitation of health; and the obligation of States parties progressively to achieve the full realisation of these rights (Article 24);
> - the right of children in care or other protection or who are receiving treatment for their physical or mental health to periodic reviews of that treatment or care/protection arrangements (Article 25);
> - the right of every child to benefit from social security, including social insurance; and the obligation on States parties to take the necessary measures to achieve the full realisation of this right in accordance with national law (article 26);
> - the right of every child to a standard of living adequate for the child's physical, mental, spiritual, moral, and social development (Article 27);
> - the right of the child to education, and in particular to primary education, which should be compulsory and available to all (Article 28);
> - the rights of children of ethnic, religious, or linguistic minorities and persons of indigenous origin to enjoy their own culture, practise their religion, and use their own language (Article 30);
> - the right of children to enjoy rest and leisure and to participate fully in cultural and artistic life (Article 31);
> - the right of the child to be protected from exploitation (Article 32).

NGO action under the CRC

In producing the second periodic report, the Labour government's approach was significantly more open and collaborative than was the case during preparation of the initial report under the previous government. Early in 1998, the Department of Health established an advisory group, comprising representatives from all relevant departments and NGO representation from England, Scotland, Wales, and Northern Ireland. The government then published a draft report in October 1998 which was circulated widely for comment, prior to final submission in September 1999.

When the government launched the process, more than 70 NGOs collaborated in producing a 'Progress Report', documenting their shared observations on the government's record in implementing the recommendations of the CRC Committee. In October 1998, the Children's Rights Office – now superseded by the broader Children's Rights Alliance – co-ordinated a further joint response on behalf of more than 50 NGOs. However, the government has largely ignored these reports, and the Alliance argues that the current report is little more than an uncritical review of aspects of government policy relating to children.

International Labour Organisation

The International Labour Organisation (ILO), founded in 1919, is a specialised agency of the UN which seeks the promotion of social justice and internationally recognised human rights and labour rights. It formulates international labour standards in the form of Conventions and Recommendations.

The ILO accomplishes its work through three main bodies, all of which are composed of representatives of government, employers, and workers. They are the International Labour Conference, the Governing Body of the ILO, and the International Labour Office. The International Labour Conference, meeting once a year, acts as an international forum for the discussion of issues relating to social and labour rights, and adopts international labour standards. This is in addition to thrice-yearly meetings of the Governing Body, which makes decisions on ILO policy.

The ILO has adopted 181 Conventions and 188 Recommendations covering a wide range of issues, including freedom of association (ILO Convention 87 (1948)); the right to organise and bargain collectively (ILO Convention 98 (1949)); equal pay for work of equal value (ILO Convention 100 (1951)); the elimination of discrimination in employment (ILO Convention 111 (1958)); and the minimum age for employment and work (ILO Convention 138 (1973)). Reservations are not permitted under the ILO process, although some Conventions provide for the partial ratification or progressive application of their provisions.

Although the UK has ratified a large number of ILO conventions, it has been widely criticised for non-compliance. However, the government has most recently ratified Convention No.111 on discrimination in employment, Convention No.138 regarding minimum age for employment, and the Convention 182 on the elimination of the worst forms of child labour. These measures have been welcomed by NGOs.

Every two years, States Parties are required to submit reports to the International Labour Office relating to the fundamental human rights Conventions,[123] plus Conventions relating to employment policy,[124] labour inspection,[125] agricultural labour inspection,[126] and tripartite consultation.[127] Reports on the other Conventions are normally required on a five-yearly basis. Governments are under an obligation to send copies of these reports to recognised workers' and employers' organisations. The following bodies are involved in the monitoring procedure:

- **The Committee of Experts on the Application of Conventions and Recommendations** examines States parties' reports and may make observations, which are published in the Committee of Experts' report (and normally relate to more serious or extended instances of non-compliance). Or it may make direct, unpublished requests to the govern-ment concerned (these normally relate to minor discrepancies). The active participation of workers' and employers' organisations in this process is encouraged.

- **The Conference Committee on the Application of Conventions and Recommendations** examines the Committee of Experts' observations on States Parties' compliance during each annual session. These discussions are summarised in the Conference Committee's report to the ILO Conference, which, after adoption, will be sent to the relevant governments.

As for a complaints procedure, the following provisions are made.

- Article 24 of the ILO Constitution allows any national or international workers' or employers' organisation to make a representation to the International Labour Office, claiming that a State Party has failed to apply an ILO Convention.

- Section 26 of the ILO Constitution allows ILO member states, ILO Conference delegates, and the Governing Body to make a complaint on the basis that a State Party is not satisfactorily securing the effective application of an ILO Convention which it has ratified. This procedure tends to be used only in cases where the regular supervisory mechanism has not been an adequate way of thoroughly examining a particular case of non-compliance.

- There are special mechanisms for supervising the application of the principles of freedom of association relating to ILO Conventions 87 and 98, based on complaints received from Member States and workers' and employers' organisations.

Summary

The UN entities with mandates covering ESC rights offer a wealth of opportunities for NGO action. NGOs with legal expertise may submit complaints to those bodies competent to examine them, or offer assistance to individuals to do so. NGOs may also make written and oral submissions to the treaty-monitoring bodies whenever the UK government's periodic reports are due for examination.

6 Developing NGO advocacy on ESC rights: recommendations

Oxfam and JUSTICE believe that non-government organisations (NGOs) have a vital role to play in promoting ESC rights in Britain, within both the voluntary sector and the wider structures of society. Indeed, many NGOs are currently engaged in a variety of such activities. With the recent implementation of the Human Rights Act (HRA) and consequent media attention paid to human rights, there has never been a better time for NGOs either to begin working to promote ESC rights or to increase their work in this area.

Oxfam and JUSTICE argue that NGOs should support the successful implementation of the HRA. Promoting the implementation and protection of ESC rights depends to a considerable degree on the success of the HRA, which should over time transform the attitudes of government bodies and public authorities. The harmonisation of domestic law and practice with other international instruments is an important objective which will need to be approached strategically and selectively.

Below are some suggestions for NGO activity, based on the material covered in this report. They constitute four main types:

- promoting ratification of key human rights instruments;
- monitoring and supervision of UK compliance with international human rights instruments;
- encouraging reviews and harmonisation of domestic law and policy, using international standards as a framework;
- lobbying and dissemination of information.

Overall, Oxfam and JUSTICE recommend that the NGO sector should seek to develop a common agenda, based on the central notion that poverty and social exclusion represent a denial of economic and social rights, and as such a denial of all human rights. NGOs should promote the development of effective structures for ensuring UK compliance with ESC rights instruments and the establishment of appropriate mechanisms for scrutiny.

There are several obstacles preventing NGOs from engaging in work to promote ESC rights either at all, or at an accelerated pace. These include lack of experience and training, especially in respect of European and international law. We suggest that NGOs should develop their expertise and their activities significantly in relation to ESC rights, in the light of the core principle that poverty and social exclusion represent a denial of human rights.

Developing mechanisms for protection

- **Building on the Human Rights Act 1998:** The implementation of the HRA marks a significant positive shift in the status of human rights in the UK. It will also provide an immediate and accessible mechanism for protecting ESC rights. Although the HRA focuses primarily on civil and political rights, it also has some implications for ESC rights (see Chapter 3). NGOs have a significant role to play in working towards full implementation of the Act, and promoting publicly the indivisibility, interdependence, and equality of *all* human rights. This could be furthered by litigation, by way of test cases and interventions, as well as by way of human rights advocacy designed to influence key Ministers and officials, related parliamentary groups, and relevant media and educational bodies.

- **The creation of an independent Human Rights Commission for the United Kingdom** remains an important goal, and NGOs should continue to campaign for it. However, there are several options to be explored, and there is no consensus on what should be the remit, powers, and structures of a Human Rights Commission.[128] NGOs should monitor closely the developments in Northern Ireland, where the government has established a Human Rights Commission which has recommended the inclusion of ESC rights in a Bill of Rights for Northern Ireland.

- **Parliamentary Joint Human Rights Committee:** The terms of reference for this committee permit it to consider and report on human rights in the UK (excluding individual cases).[129] Since its establishment in January 2001, it has initiated an inquiry into the case for a UK Human Rights Commission and scrutinised the human rights aspects of a range of government bills (especially the Criminal Justice and Police Bill). NGOs should seek to ensure that the Committee accords sufficient importance to the monitoring and implementation of ESC rights.

- **The European Union:** The treaties of the European Union provide direct authority for the protection of some ESC rights. This makes the EU a significant forum in which to secure protection for such rights. There is potentially an important role for NGOs to play at EU level in monitoring legal and political change and shaping EU policy, either through direct contact with the European Commission or the European Parliament, or in conjunction with pan-European umbrella groups (in sectors such as poverty and social exclusion, the environment, disability, migration, and child care). In addition, NGOs should remain alert to opportunities for lobbying at the UK level on EU matters, because national governments hold ultimate power within the EU structures through their membership of the Council of Ministers.

Promoting ratification of key ESC-rights instruments

- **Revised European Social Charter and the Additional Protocol:** The Council of Europe's Revised Social Charter of 1996 encompasses a wide range of social and economic rights, tailored to fit the European context. The UK has ratified the original 1961 Social Charter and has signed the Revised Social Charter (which includes a wider range of rights, for example in relation to employment, housing, poverty, and social exclusion). It stated in 1998 that it was 'actively considering which articles it might ratify',[130] and the FCO Annual Human Rights Report for 2000 stated that the government would ratify it 'in due course'. But the government has neither signed nor ratified the 1995 Additional Protocol, which provides for a system of collective complaints and allows certain NGOs (and employers and trade unions) to file complaints. NGOs should therefore call for the UK government to announce a timetable for full ratification of the Revised Social Charter and the Additional Protocol.

- **ECHR Additional Protocol 12:** The adoption of Additional Protocol 12 will, once it receives the requisite number of ratifications, add a free-standing non-discrimination provision to the European Convention on Human Rights. It opened for signature and ratification in November 2000. The NGO sector should work with other groups to persuade the government to ratify and incorporate the Additional Protocol. JUSTICE is taking a lead on this issue.

- **Moving towards an Optional Protocol to the International Covenant on ESC rights:** The Covenant is a useful tool for UK NGOs, protecting a wide range of social, economic, and cultural rights. As yet there is no complaints procedure, but the possible development of an Optional Protocol to provide for this is being examined at the international level by an independent expert appointed by the Commission on Human Rights. The UK government has stated that it does not yet have a view on this, but that it is playing an active role in the discussions.[131] NGOs should encourage the government to take a more positive stance, and should continue to lobby the UN for the adoption of an Optional Protocol.

Monitoring and supervision

- **Responding to UK government periodic reports:** NGOs can play an important role in helping to monitor the UK government's compliance with its international obligations under ESC rights instruments. This can be achieved by responding to the UK government's periodic reports and by making submissions to the appropriate supervisory bodies of particular instruments. Although there are clearly instances where individual NGOs have special expertise and where they may wish to act independently, there are also significant advantages in undertaking joint submissions. The compilation of a single NGO 'parallel report' provides a focus for lobbying activity, and encourages the sharing of knowledge, skills, and resources among organisations. It is therefore suggested that NGOs should work together on the production of parallel reports under the European Social

Charter and the International Covenant on Economic, Social and Cultural Rights. Joint working in relation to ICERD, CEDAW, ILO, and the CRC should also be strengthened.

- **Ensuring that UK government reports are disseminated and debated:** NGOs should seek to ensure that UK government reports under ESC rights instruments are tabled in Parliament prior to submission to the supervisory body, published with a press release, and made available in appropriate formats (including the government's official web-site) to all tiers of government, public bodies, NGOs, and libraries. The instigation of similar processes in relation to the concluding observations of supervisory bodies should also be encouraged. Alongside such dissemination, NGOs should call for the UK government to initiate conferences, workshops, and seminars, linked to media strategies, to stimulate national debate concerning ESC rights.

Encouraging reviews and harmonisation of domestic law and policy with international human rights standards

- **ESC rights audits:** Given that the HRA applies to public bodies and NGOs, such organisations will need to audit their existing policies and practice to ensure compliance. As part of this process, NGOs should seek to ensure that these audits extend beyond the basic requirements of the HRA, incorporating the standards of the key ESC-rights instruments. These provisions (and the recommendations made by supervisory bodies) should be used as a framework for developing policy and practice, both within and beyond their organisations.

- **Adoption of international instruments:** NGOs should formally adopt the Revised Social Charter and/or the ICESCR as an expression of their commitment to the principles, and then use these instruments as a tool to audit policy and practice. They should also encourage public authorities to do the same. A similar approach has been employed in the UK by the Children's Rights Office, which has been successful in persuading more than 400 local authorities to 'adopt' the UN Convention on the Rights of the Child.

- **Reviewing UK reservations to ESC rights instruments, especially the European Social Charter:** The government announced the outcome of its review of the UK's position under international human rights instruments on 3 March 1999. This has resulted in some positive advances in relation to ESC rights (such as the withdrawal of the reservation on Article 32 of the CRC,[132] and its intention to ratify the Council of Europe's Revised Social Charter).

No significant changes were recommended in relation to existing reservations to ICESCR, ICERD, or CEDAW. NGOs should recommend that a detailed review should examine UK reservations to ESC rights instruments. In relation to the European Social Charter, which was not addressed in the government's review, the UK's failure to accept certain provisions under Articles 2 (reasonable daily and weekly working hours), 4 (equal pay for work of equal value), and 7 and 8 (protection for young people and women in employment) should be addressed.

- **Further action to assess UK compliance with ESC-rights instruments:** NGOs should argue that when the government is preparing a submission to the supervisory bodies of the ESC-rights instruments – and especially the European Social Charter and the International Covenant on Economic, Social and Cultural Rights – comprehensive reviews should be undertaken of UK domestic law and policy, to assess compliance with the relevant articles of these instruments. In-depth assessments should be made within the review processes to ascertain whether any new laws or codes should be adopted, or amendments introduced in domestic legislation and guidance, to ensure compliance and implementation. Such reviews could be undertaken by independent experts and submitted to Parliament for discussion and debate.

Lobbying and dissemination of information and material

- **Dissemination of information to individuals and civil society:** NGOs should design appropriate strategies and materials for raising awareness among individuals and civil society (for example schools, church groups, or special-interest groups) about key issues in relation to ESC rights, and they should explore innovative methods for disseminating such information. NGOs should also encourage the development of education on human rights within the national curriculum (and especially as part of compulsory education in citizenship from 2002), and seek to ensure that such education stresses the indivisibility of human rights and the importance of ESC rights.

- **Developing continuing consultation between the UK government and NGOs on ESC rights:** To ensure wider participation in the supervisory processes of ESC rights instruments and assist the promotion of a 'human rights culture', NGOs should seek to establish on-going mechanisms (possibly operating through an informal coalition) for engaging with the UK government and devolved administrations on ESC rights.

- **Promoting ESC rights in devolved administrations:** In addition to developing a set of proposals for Whitehall and Westminster, NGOs should develop a similar agenda to ensure the mainstreaming of ESC rights within the administrations in Scotland, Wales, and Northern Ireland. It is important that NGOs should initiate UK-wide activities and links, and build on the experience that is emerging from Scotland, Wales, and Northern Ireland.

- **Developing UK NGO activity in relation to the Council of Europe:** International NGOs (with consultative status with the Council of Europe) and trade unions and organisations of employers all have powers under the Social Charter to gain access to information and to make an input into the supervision process. However, national NGOs at present have no formal place. They should lobby key bodies within the Council of Europe – in conjunction with international organisations – for improved access and consultation rights. NGOs operating at the European level, especially those who may be interested in lodging complaints under the Collective Complaints Protocol (following ratification by the UK government), should consider applying for consultative status with the Council of Europe. More generally, UK NGOs should support moves to raise the status of social rights in relevant Council of Europe forums.

Appendix: Procedures and addresses for UN and ILO mechanisms[133]

1 Committee on Economic, Social and Cultural Rights

Members: 18 members meet twice a year for sessions of three working weeks, and one week with a working group.

Reports: annually to UN Economic and Social Council (ECOSOC).

Procedure:
- Government submits report.
- NGOs make submissions.
- NGOs may apply to make oral submissions at the beginning of the pre-sessional working group. NGOs may suggest questions to put forward to the government.
- One member of the pre-sessional working group takes responsibility for each country reporting (preparing a draft list of issues to be considered by the pre-sessional working group and drafting the Committee's concluding observations).
- NGOs may apply to make oral submissions on the first afternoon of the session.
- The country report is considered during three-hour meetings during the session.
- Committee meets in private to consider its concluding observations.
- Periodic reports every five years.

Days of general discussion: one day per session enables the Committee to encourage contributions to its work from all interested parties.

Missions:
- Committee indicates its desire to have its representatives invited to visit a State Party to collect information necessary for the Committee to properly review the implementation of Covenant in the country.
- NGOs convey relevant information to the Secretariat to assist it and the Committee members to create an appropriate mission programme.

Exceptional action: NGOs communicate information of an urgent nature to the Committee, requesting its rapid response.

Deadline for submissions: at least two months before the date set for discussion of periodic report.

Contact: The Secretary (Mr Alexandre Tikhonov), Office of the UN High Commissioner for Human Rights, Palais des Nations, 1211 Geneva 10, Switzerland, Tel. 00 41 22 917 3968; fax 00 41 22 917 0099.

2 Committee on the Elimination of Discrimination Against Women (CEDAW)

Members: 23 elected by the States Parties for four-year terms. Meets twice a year in New York for three weeks.

Reports to: General Assembly, via ECOSOC annually.

Procedure:
- Government submits report.
- NGOs make submissions.
- Government presents report at hearing.
- Committee makes general comments on report.
- Committee asks questions on individual articles in CEDAW.
- Government replies.
- Final comments by Committee members.
- Periodic reports every four years.

Deadline for submissions: two months before the date set for discussion of periodic report.

Contact: The Secretary (Ms Jane Connors), Division for the Advancement of Women, PO Box 20, United Nations, New York, NY 10017, USA. Tel. 00 1 212 963 3162; fax 00 1 212 963 3463.

3 Committee on the Elimination of Racial Discrimination (CERD)

Members: 18 members elected by the States Parties for four-year terms, with half the Committee standing down every two years.

Reports to: General Assembly, via Secretary General annually

Procedure:
- Government submits report.
- NGOs make submissions.
- Government presents report at hearing.
- Country Rapporteur asks questions.
- Other Committee members ask questions, considering admissibility and merits of complaints.
- Government replies.
- Final comments by Committee members.
- Closed session to consider views.
- Public expression of Committee's views.
- Periodic reports every two years.

Deadline for submissions: two months before the date set for discussion of periodic report.

Contact: The Secretary (M. MacDarrow), Committee on the Elimination of Racial Discrimination, Office of the High Commissioner for Human Rights, Palais des Nations, 1211 Geneva 10, Switzerland. Tel. 00 41 22 917 9439; fax 00 41 22 917 9022.

4 Committee on the Rights of the Child (CRC)

Members: ten members elected by States Parties for four-year terms. Meets three times a year (January, May-June, September-October) for sessions of three working weeks and a one-week meeting of a working group to prepare for the following session.

Reports to: General Assembly, via ECOSOC every two years.

Procedure:
- Government submits report.
- Secretariat prepares country analysis.
- NGOs, relevant UN bodies, and specialised agencies make submissions.
- Pre-sessional working group of the CRC meets in private to prepare for next session. It receives input from NGOs, relevant UN bodies, and specialised agencies and draws up a list of issues to address to reporting governments.
- Governments are requested to supply written answers to the list of issues before the session.
- Government presents report at the session.
- Country Rapporteur(s) and other CRC members ask questions.
- Government replies.
- CRC members make preliminary oral observations.
- CRC meets in private to draft concluding observations in writing.
- CRC's observations are adapted in public during the final meeting of the season.
- Periodic reports every five years.

Missions: two/three participants alert the Committee to particular national problems.

Urgent situations: NGOs may bring emergency instances of human-rights violations to the attention of the Committee.

Deadline for submissions: two months before the date set for discussion of periodic report in pre-sessional working group.

Contact: The Secretary (Mr Paulo David), Office of the UN High Commissioner for Human Rights, Palais des Nations, 1211 Geneva 10, Switzerland. Tel. 00 41 22 917 9301; fax. 00 41 22 917 9022.

5 International Labour Organisation

The Committee of Experts on the Application of Conventions and Recommendations

Members: appointed by the Director-General for renewable three-year periods. Meets in private on dates determined by the governing body.

Report: published in March and immediately sent to governments. Direct requests concerning submission to the competent authorities (as well as observations, which are already published in the report of the Committee) are transmitted together with the memorandum on submission.

Procedure:
- Committee assigns to each of its members initial responsibility for groups of Conventions or subjects.
- Reports and information received early enough by the Office are forwarded to the member concerned before the session.
- To deal with general or particularly complex questions, the Committee appoints working parties, which then submit their findings to the Committee as a whole.
- Documentation available to the Committee includes the information supplied by governments in their reports or in the Conference Committee on the application of standards.
- Conclusions of the Committee traditionally represent unanimous agreement among its members, although any dissent and response from the Committee are included in its Report.
- A qualified secretariat is placed at the Committee's disposal by the Director-General of the ILO.
- The report of the Committee is submitted to the governing body.

The final findings take the following form:

- Part 1: a general report, giving an overview of the Committee's work and drawing the attention of the Governing Body, the Conferences, and Member States to matters of general interest and concern.
- Part 2: individual observations on the application of ratified Conventions in Member States; the application of Conventions in non-metropolitan territories for whose international relations Member States are responsible; and the submission of Recommendations to the national competent authorities; a series of direct requests; a series of acknowledgements.
- Part 3: a general survey of national law and practice with regard to the instruments on which reports have been supplied on unratified Conventions and on Recommendations under article 19 of the Constitution.

Conference Committee on the Application of Conventions and Recommendations

Issues: Governments are able to amplify information previously supplied; indicate further measures proposed; draw attention to difficulties met with in the discharge of obligations, and seek guidance on how to overcome such difficulties.

Members: tripartite composition, consisting of representatives of governments, employers, and workers.

Procedure:
- The Committee considers the Report of the Committee of Experts. It also considers documents containing the substance of written replies to observations of the Committee of Experts and supplementary information received by the Office since the meeting of the Committee of Experts.
- The Committee discusses the general survey in the report and individual cases. A summary of governments' statements and the ensuing discussion is reproduced in an appendix to the Committee's report to the Conference.
- The Committee's report is presented to the Conference and discussed in plenary, which gives delegates a further opportunity to draw attention to particular aspects of the Committee's work.
- The report is published in the Record of Proceedings of the Conference and separately for circulation to governments.

Contact: Director-General, International Labour Office, 4, route des Morillons, CH-1211 Geneva 22, Switzerland. Tel: 41 22 799 6019; fax: 41 22 799 8533.

Glossary

Committee of Ministers of the Council of Europe The Committee is the decision-making body of the Council of Europe. It consists of the ministers of foreign affairs of the Member States, now numbering more than 40. See **Council of Europe.**

Community Charter of Fundamental Social Rights of Workers 1989 A non-binding EU charter of basic social rights for workers. It includes employment and pay, living and working conditions, the protection of young people at work, and protection for the elderly and people with disabilities. Sometimes referred to as the Social Charter, or the Community Charter. Not to be confused with the EU Charter of Fundamental Rights and Freedoms or the Council of Europe's European Social Charter.

Concluding Observations A monitoring committee's decision on whether or not a State's legislation or practice complies with the provisions of a treaty.

Consultative Status Status granted by the UN or Council of Europe to certain NGOs which are representative in their field of competence. It allows those institutions to consult the NGOs on issues of mutual interest.

Council of Europe A European inter-government organisation, based in Strasbourg. Its main role is to strengthen democracy, human rights, and the rule of law throughout its Member States in Europe. With over 40 members, since 1989 it has become the main political focus for co-operation with the countries of central and eastern Europe. Not to be confused with European Union or European Community.
See also **Committee of Ministers, Parliamentary Assembly, European Court of Human Rights, and European Social Charter.**

Council of Ministers of the European Union A European Union institution, consisting of government representatives of the 15 Member States. The Council has the ultimate legislative power within the EU. Sometimes referred to as the European Council.

Beyond Civil Rights

European Commission A European Union institution which initiates and promotes Community legislation and proposes policies to flow from the provisions of treaties. It seeks to ensure that Member States comply with Community legislation (and, as a last resort, it can institute breach proceedings before the ECJ). It acts as mediator when inter-government disputes arise. Commissioners are appointed by Member States.

European Court of Human Rights (EctHR) A Council of Europe institution. An independent judicial body which hears individual cases of alleged violation of the European Convention on Human Rights by a Contracting-Party. The Court has the power to bind Member States to carry out its decisions. Not to be confused with the European Court of Justice.

European Court of Justice (ECJ) An EU institution, the ECJ seeks to ensure that EU law is observed in the interpretation and application of the Treaties, and generally, in all of the activities of the Union. The ECJ cannot hear cases brought by individual citizens. Not to be confused with the European Court of Human Rights.

European Parliament An EU institution, directly elected by the citizens of the European Union. It does not have legislative powers in the same way as a national parliament, because most important EU law is made by the Council of Ministers. However, very few texts can be adopted without the Parliament's opinion having been sought. The Parliament also adopts the EU's budget every year.

European Social Charter A Council of Europe human rights treaty by which Contracting Parties agree to protect and promote ESC rights. Not to be confused with the EU Social Chapter of the Treaty of Amsterdam, or the EU Community Charter of Social Rights of Workers 1989.

European Union The European Union is a development of the 'European Community'. Following the 1991 Maastricht Treaty, the European Community became one of three pillars of European Union (the others being foreign and security policy, and justice and home affairs). These latter activities are largely conducted on an inter-government basis. Not to be confused with the Council of Europe. See also Council of Ministers, European Commission, European Court of Justice, European Parliament.

Member States	Governments who belong to an international or European organisation, e.g. Member States of the Council of Europe.
Periodic Report	A report made at regular intervals by a government to one of the Committees that monitor human rights treaties. In the report the government must explain how it has implemented the relevant treaty.
Parliamentary Assembly	A Council of Europe institution. A deliberative body consisting of representatives appointed by the national Parliaments of each Member State. Not to be confused with the European Parliament of the EU.
Protocol	An addition to a human rights treaty.
Ratification	The process whereby a government agrees to be bound by a treaty.
Respondent State	A government against whom a complaint has been made under an international treaty to a monitoring committee or court.
Signature	The preliminary means by which a State endorses a treaty but is not yet bound by it.
Social Chapter/Social Protocol	Refers to the social-policy provisions of the EU Treaty of Amsterdam 1997. It is the successor to the Protocol on Social Policy and Agreement on Social Policy, which were the result of a disagreement between the UK and other Member States over the inclusion of social-policy provisions in the earlier Treaty of Maastricht. Not to be confused with The European Social Charter, or the Community Charter of Fundamental Social Rights of Workers 1989, or the EU Charter of Fundamental Rights and Freedoms.

Notes

1. Foreign and Commonwealth Office and Department for International Development, 'Human Rights', Annual Report for 1999, Cm 4404.
2. Foreign and Commonwealth Office and Department for International Development, 'Human Rights', Annual Report for 2000, Cm 4774.
3. Resolution 55/106, adopted by the UN General Assembly, 'Human Rights and Extreme Poverty', A/RES/55/106 of 14 March 2001.
4. For further information, see the website http://www.atd.demon.co.uk
5. Commission on the NHS (2000) *New Life for Health*, Vintage Original.
6. RES (1999) *NI Social Omnibus Survey*.
7. Figures taken from *Poverty and Social Exclusion in Britain*, David Gordon et al., Rowntree Foundation, 2000.
8. European Anti-Poverty Network (1999) 'A Europe for All: For a European Strategy to Combat Social Exclusion', www.eapn.org
9. Commission on Poverty, Participation, and Power (2000) *Listen Hear: The Right to be Heard*, The Policy Press.
10. C. Ferguson (1999) 'Global Social Policy Principles: Human Rights and Social Justice', Department for International Development.
11. Statement by Mary Robinson, United Nations High Commissioner for Human Rights, at the Special Dialogue on Poverty and the Enjoyment of Human Rights, Commission on Human Rights, 56th session, 12 April 2000.
12. The other participants were the Children's Rights Office, Disability Alliance Educational and Research Association, Disability Awareness in Action, European Anti-Poverty Network, Low Pay Unit, National Council for One Parent Families, 1990 Trust, Parity, Runnymede Trust, Refugee Council, and Shelter.
13. Presentation at Oxfam/JUSTICE seminar, London.
14. Francesca Klug has recently challenged the classification of 'first' and 'second' generation rights, arguing that this creates an excessively rigid distinction between these categories, whereas in fact ideas flow between them. See F. Klug (2000) *Values for a Godless Age: The Story of the UK's New Bill of Rights*, Penguin.
15. See Glossary.
16. Harmondsworth: Penguin, 2000.
17. Paul Hunt (1996) *Reclaiming Social Justice: International and Comparative Perspectives*, Dartmouth Publishing, Chapters 2 and 5.
18. Professor Stein Evju, Vice-President of the European Committee of Social Rights, 'Applying the European Social Charter within the National Legal System', speech to conference on Fundamental Social Rights in Northern Ireland, Belfast, 17 June 1999.
19. David Matas, 'Economic, social and cultural rights and the role of lawyers: North American Perspectives' in The International Commission of Jurists Bangalore Conference Report 1995, *Economic, Social and Cultural Rights and the Role of Lawyers*.
20. Matthew Craven (1999) 'The justiciability of economic social and cultural rights' in Burchill, Harris, and Owers (eds) *Economic Social and Cultural Rights: Their Implementation in United Kingdom Human Rights Law* (Nottingham University); and Paul Hunt, op.cit., p.26.
21. Harmondsworth: Penguin, 1999.
22. UN Committee on ESC Rights, General Comment No 3, para. 10, UN Document E/1991/23.
23. Our emphasis.
24. Our emphasis.
25. General Comment no.7 E/C.12/1997/4, 20 May 1997.
26. Brown v. The Board of Education 347 U.S. 483 (1954).
27. All-Party Oireachtas Committee on the Constitution, 'Report of the Review Group on the Constitution' (1996).
28. Northern Ireland Human Rights

Commission (2000) 'Social and Economic Rights', www.nihrc.org
29　Ibid., p. 235.
30　A Commission of the Irish Catholic Bishops' Conference.
31　'Re-righting the Constitution. The Case for New Social and Economic Rights: Housing, Health, Nutrition, Adequate standard of living' (1998).
32　However, on occasion the courts have used the Article 45 principles to inform their interpretation of personal rights under Article 40.3 (for example, Murtagh Properties v Cleary [1972] IR 330, Rogers v ITGWU, unreported, 15 March 1978 – the right to earn a livelihood).
33　Matthew Craven. See note 20 above.
34　National Coalition for Gay and Lesbian Equality and others v Minister of Home Affairs and Others, 2000(1) BCLR 39.
35　1997] 12 BCLR 1696.
36　Ibid., P. Chaskalson, para. 29.
37　CESC Ltd. v. Subash Chandra [1992] 1 SCC 441.
38　Olga Tellis v. Bombay Municipal Corp [1985] 2 Supp SCR 51 (India).
39　Mohini Jain v. State of Karnataka JT [1992] 4 SC 292 (India).
40　Charan Lal Sahu v. Union of India 1990 (1) SCC 687 (Bhopal Gas Disaster case). The Court held that the right to life and liberty included pollution-free air and water.
41　See the Maastricht Guidelines on Violations of ESC rights, SIM Special No 20, 1977.
42　See above, note 28.
43　See above, note 28, p. 359.
44　Ozgur Gundem v Turkey, Judgment of 16 March 2000, Application No. 23144/93.
45　UN Document E/CN.4/1987/17. See also *Human Rights Quarterly* 9 (1987), pp. 122-35.
46　See Sim Special No 20 (1997) pp. 1-12, and V. Dankwa, C. Flinterman and S. Leckie: 'Commentary to the Maastricht Guidelines on Violations of Economic Social and Cultural Rights', *Human Rights Quarterly* 20 (1998), pp.705-30.
47　CESCR General Comment No. 3 UN Doc. E/1991/23 and 'The Limburg Principles on the Implementation of the Covenant on Economic, Social and Cultural Rights'.
48　CESCR General Comment No 3 UN Doc. E/1991/23, para. 10.
49　The Maastricht Guidelines, para. 10.
50　The Maastricht Guidelines, para. 9.
51　D. Selbourne (1994) *The Principle of Duty*, London: Sinclair Stevenson.
52　International Council on Human Rights (1999) 'Taking Duties Seriously: Individual Duties in International Human Rights Law'.
53　T. Hammerberg (1999) 'The Principles and Politics of Human Rights', Dorab Patel Lecture, London School of Economics, 18 February 1999.
54　In the UK, a rights-based approach to welfare was still visible in the Labour Party's approach to welfare until relatively recently: Labour Party, *Jobs and Social Justice* (1994).
55　All-Party Parliamentary Group on Poverty (1999) First Report of the APPG.
56　'New Ambitions for our Country: A New Contract for Welfare' (1998), Cm 3805.
57　It should be noted that the HRA also has significant implications for NGOs – especially those that are deemed 'public authorities' under the Act – in relation to issues such as service provision and employment practice. These areas are not considered within the scope of this report. For further information, see National Council for Voluntary Organisations (2000), *Impact of the Human Rights Act on Voluntary Organisations*.
58　Foreign Secretary, speech to the Amnesty International Human Rights Festival, London, 16 October 1998.
59　International Development Secretary, speech to special session of the UN General Assembly, New York, 10 December 1998.
60　Foreign and Commonwealth Office and Department for International Development, 'Human Rights', Annual Report for 2000, Cm 4774, p. 72.
61　Foreign and Commonwealth Office and Department for International Development, 'Human Rights', Annual Report for 1999, Cm 4404, p.15.
62　Foreign and Commonwealth Office and Department for International Development, 'Human Rights', Annual Report for 2000, Cm 4774, p. 72.
63　Foreign and Commonwealth Office and Department for International Development, 'Human Rights', Annual Report for 1999, Cm 4404, p16.
64　T. Kenny (1997) 'Securing Social Rights Across Europe: how NGOs can make use of the European Social Charter', Oxfam GB.
65　Replies were due by 30 June 2001.
66　Based on the FCO and Department for

International Development, Human Rights' Annual Report 1999, Cm 4404, and FCO Human Rights Annual Report 2000, Cm 4774.
67 The prohibition of forced labour is found both in Article 4 of the ECHR and in Article 1(2) of the European Social Charter. There are links between Articles 2 and 3 of the ECHR on the right to life and protection against 'inhuman and degrading treatment', and Article 3 of the European Social Charter on the right to safe and healthy working conditions. There is also a clear relationship between Article 11 of the ECHR on freedom of association and Article 5 of the European Social Charter on the right to organise. In addition, there is a link with Article 6 of the European Social Charter on the right to bargain collectively. Protection of the family is covered in Article 8 of the ECHR and Article 16 of the European Social Charter (as well as other provisions, such as Article 19 on migrant workers and their families).
68 Section 2(1) HRA 1998.
69 For further reading, see JUSTICE and The Public Law Project: 'A Matter of Public Interest: reforming the law and practice on interventions in public interest cases' (1996).
70 A successful example is the intervention by JUSTICE in the House of Lords and the ECtHR in the case of Thompson and Venables, the two boys convicted of murdering James Bulger. JUSTICE presented material on the compatibility of the treatment of juveniles in the criminal justice system with the Convention on the Rights of the Child, and with practice in other European countries. Further examples of interventions before the ECtHR include the intervention by the TUC before the ECtHR in a case concerning the trades union closed-shop rule and by MIND in a case to provide information on conditions in mental hospitals and patients' rights.
71 Anti-discrimination legislation in Northern Ireland is covered by the Race Relations (Northern Ireland) Order 1997 and the Northern Ireland Act 1998 (which do prohibit religious discrimination).
72 JUSTICE, 'Asylum and Immigration Bill: Human Rights Compliance', Evidence to the House of Commons Special Standing Committee (March 1999).
73 J. Wadham and H. Mountfield (1999) *Human Rights Act 1998*, Blackstone.
74 [1998] EHRLR 354.
75 Cornwall v UK (application no 36578/97), Leary v UK (application no 38890/97), Crossland v UK (application no 36120/97).
76 Wadham and Mountfield, op. cit.
77 An exception is made, however, for decisions on matters of immigration or nationality, where appropriately authorised, and for decisions not to institute criminal proceedings.
78 Affaire Salgueiro da Silva Mouta v. Portugal case no 33290/96 21.12.99.
79 N v. UK no. 11077/84 49 DR 170.
80 Inze v. Austria A 126 (1988) 10 EHRR 394 and Marckx v Belgium A31 (1979) 2 EHRR 330.
81 Rasmussen v Denmark A 87 (1985) 7 EHRR 352.
82 National Union of Belgium Police v Belgium A 19 (1975) 1 EHRR 578.
83 Airey v Ireland (1979–1980) 2 EHRR 305.
84 25 November 2000.
85 It is worth making the distinction here between the European Union and the Council of 85 Europe. The EU (sometimes referred to as the European Economic Community, the European Community, or the Common Market) has 15 Member States and its main objective is the creation of a single integrated market. However, it has extended its competence to act in areas of social protection, home affairs, security, and defence. The Council of Europe has over 40 Member States, including all EU Member States, and is a European inter-governmental organisation based in Strasbourg. It is responsible for the promotion of democracy, human rights, and the rule of law throughout its Member States.
86 The Treaty of Amsterdam has changed the numbering of the EC Treaty. This is now Article 141.
87 Prior to this amendment, the powers of the EU as a whole to engage in social-policy making were very limited; after the Maastricht Treaty (or Treaty of European Union of 1992), the EU was split between the 11 States that agreed to the Protocol on Social Policy, and the United Kingdom, which did not ratify the Protocol. Directives adopted in respect of social policy pursuant to the Protocol therefore did not apply to

the UK. The Treaty of Amsterdam (1997) scrapped the Protocol and incorporated its provisions into the EC Treaty. The effect of this is that from then on, all EU Member States are involved in and covered by the social-policy provisions.
88 See Glossary.
89 In the case of age and disability, this can be extended to 2 December 2006.
90 Article 6 of the Treaty of European Union.
91 See Glossary
92 There is an EU Regulation 1612/68, which provides for equal access to housing for migrant workers.
93 Comité des Sages, 'For a Europe of Civic and Social Rights' (1995) European Commission, Brussels.
94 Charte 4487/1/00REV 1, Brussels, 10 October 2000.
95 Information about the work programmes of the committees is available on the Parliament website (www.parliament.uk).
96 The Commission consists of various Directorates-General, each with responsibility for a discrete policy area.
97 The European Parliament may be effectively lobbied by targeting the relevant Parliamentary Committee (for instance, the Committee on Employment and Social Policy).
98 [1996] IRLR 347.
99 Article 230, EC Treaty.
100 Article 37, Statute of the Court of Justice.
101 See K. Lasok (1994) *The European Court of Justice: Practice and Procedure*, Butterworths Law p.168.
102 Article 20, Statute of the Court of Justice.
103 Further information may be obtained from the Council of Europe web-site: www.coe.fr/index.asp and the human rights web-site: www.dhdirhr.coe.fr
104 Cm 4774, p 150.
105 For information on the complaints system, see T. Kenny (1998) 'Securing Social Rights in Europe', Oxfam GB.
106 European Committee of Social Rights, Conclusions for the XV-1 supervision cycle, http://www.humanrights.coe.int/cseweb/GB/GB2/GB23e_UK.html
107 Council of Europe Committee of Ministers, Recommendation No. R ChS (93)3 and Recommendation No. R Chs (97)3.
108 European Committee of Social Rights, Conclusions for the XV-2 supervision cycle, http://www.humanrights.coe.int/cseweb/GB/GB2/XV2%Fact%20sheets/GB24e_UK.html
109 Committee for the Administration of Justice (1999) 'Fundamental Social Rights in Northern Ireland: Building upon the Agreement and the European Social Charter', Belfast.
110 In the chapter, the work of United Nations Special Rapporteurs (on matters such as Disabilities, and the Right to Education) are not covered in any detail. Rapporteurs (or Working Groups) investigate particular human-rights issues (for example, by undertaking fact-finding missions, and consultation with governments and NGOs) and make recommendations for action. Whereas treaty-monitoring bodies have jurisdiction only over the States Parties to a particular treaty, these 'thematic mandates' extend to all UN Member States and can refer to all relevant legal standards. Information may be sent to relevant UN Special Rapporteurs at any time.
111 For more information on monitoring procedures, see 'Human Rights Human Wrongs: a guide to the human rights machinery of the United Nations' by Jane Winter, British Irish Rights Watch, June 1996.
112 Foreign and Commonwealth Office and Department for International Development, 'Human Rights', Annual Report for 1999, Cm 4404.
113 See Chapter 2 for more on the Maastricht Guidelines and Limburg Principles.
114 Resolution 2001/30 of 20 April 2001, Commission on Human Rights
115 Concluding Observations of the Committee on Economic Social and Cultural Rights on the UK's 3rd Periodic Report E/C.12/Add.19, 4 December 1999.
116 Ibid.
117 Ibid., paragraph 11.
118 Oxfam/JUSTICE, 'Poverty Undermines Rights', October 1997.
119 E/CN.6/1999/WG/L3.
120 CEDAW/C/1999/L.2/ADD.7.
121 Concluding Observations of the Committee on the Elimination of Racial Discrimination: United Kingdom of Great Britain and Northern Ireland, 01/05/2001, CERD/C/304/Add.102.
122 CRC/C/15/ADD.34.
123 Nos. 29, 87, 98, 100, 105, 111, and 138
124 No. 122, 1964

125 No. 122, 1964
126 No. 129, 1969
127 No. 144, 1976
128 S. Spencer and I. Bynoe (1998) 'A Human Rights Commission: the options for Britain and Northern Ireland', IPPR.
129 The Committee's 12 members are drawn from both the House of Lords and House of Commons. Its terms of reference are 'to consider and report on (a) matters relating to human rights in the United Kingdom (but excluding consideration of individual cases); (b) proposals for remedial orders, draft remedial orders and remedial orders made under section 10 of and laid under Schedule 2 to the Human Rights Act 1998; (c) in respect of draft remedial orders and remedial orders, whether the special attention of the House should be drawn to them on any of the grounds specified in Standing Order 73 (Joint Committee on Statutory Instruments)'.
130 Foreign and Commonwealth Office statement to the Select Committee on Foreign Affairs, 20 October 1998
131 Written answer to Parliamentary Question, *Hansard* (HL) 5 April 2000.
132 Withdrawal of the reservation is a result of UK implementation of the EU Young Workers Directive and ratification of ILO Convention 111 on discrimination in employment.
133 This section relies heavily on Jane Winter's *Human Wrongs, Human Rights*, first published by British Irish Rights Watch in 1996 and soon to be republished by the Northern Ireland Human Rights Commission. Additional material was taken from *Human Rights and the UN*, by M O'Flaherty (Sweet and Maxwell 1996).

Index

Figures in italics indicate text in boxes.

1990 Trust *43*
accommodation
   'no choice' 3
   see also housing
African-Caribbean children,
   excluded 27, 40
age
   discrimination 25, 27
   and equality of opportunity 28, *36*
   new EU discrimination directive 4
Age Concern *31*
agricultural labour inspection 45
All-Party Parliamentary Group on
   Poverty *19*
Alston, P. and Weiler, J.H.H.:
   The European Union and
      Human Rights: Final project
      report on an agenda for the
      year 2000' 22
Amsterdam, Treaty of (1997) 29-32,
   31
anti-discrimination law 25, 27-8, 29
   advancing ESC rights 4, 23
   NGOs' role re ESC rights 4-5
'anti-social' behaviour 19
arrest, arbitrary *17*
association, freedom of 45
asylum seekers
   dispersal system 42-3
   and the HRA 3, *26*
   UKPP supports iv
ATD Fourth World 8

bank loans *41*
Beirne, Maggie *10*
Belfast Agreement (1998) 22, *24*
Belgium 35
belief
   freedom of 25
   new EU discrimination directive 4
Bill of Rights
   International 11
   New Zealand 12
   proposed for Northern Ireland
      2, 8, 22-3, *23*, 46
   proposed for UK 8, 46
'bind-over' orders on parents 4, *26-7*
Brazil: National Human Rights
   Programme 17
CAJ *see* Committee on the
   Administration of Justice
Canada: Constitution 12

Canadian Charter on Fundamental
   Rights and Freedoms 12
case law 12, 24, 25, 32, 33
CEDAW *see* Convention on the
   Elimination of Discrimination
   Against Women
CERD *see* Convention on the
   Elimination of all Forms of
   Racial Discrimination
CESCR *see* UN Committee on
   Economic, Social and Cultural
   Rights
child care 47
   Northern Ireland *36*
Child Support Agency (CSA) 4
children
   best interests of 43, *44*
   child labour 24, 35, *35*, 45
   child support 4
   commercial sexual exploitation 24
   deprived of necessities 8
   Gypsy 43
   health care 43, *44*
   poverty *40*, 43
   protection from economic and
      social exploitation *39*
   right to social, legal, and
      economic protection *34*
   right to special care and
      assistance *38*
   rights 2, 14, 17, 19, 30, 43, *44*
   supporting one's children 9
   Traveller 43
   see also Convention on the Rights
      of the Child
Children's Rights Alliance 13, 44
Children's Rights Office 44, 48
citizenship
   compulsory education on 5, 49
   and ESC rights 1
   radical redefinition of 19
civil rights *1*
   changes over time 2-3, 14
   cost of implementation 16
   examples *12*
   and the Human Rights Act v, 1,
      2, 7, 23, 28, 46
   precisely drafted 2, 13
   primacy over ESC rights 12-13
   recommendations to the civil
      and political realm *10*
   and the UDHR 11

clothing 8, 25, *39*
Cold War 11, 13, 20
collective bargaining 31, *34*, 35, *35*, 45
Comité des Sages report (1995) 30
Commission for Racial Equality
   (CRE) 27, *31*
   'The Race Relations (Amendment)
      Bill: questions and answers' *28*
Commission of Human Rights 47
Committee of Ministers 33, 35
Committee on Economic, Social
   and Cultural Rights 38, 50
Committee on the Administration
   of Justice (CAJ) *36*
Committee on the Elimination of
   Discrimination Against Women
   (CEDAW) 50
Committee on the Elimination of
   Racial Discrimination (CERD) 51
Committee on the Rights of the
   Child 43, 51
common law 37, 40
community care rights 22
Confederation of British Industry *31*
conscience, freedom of *12*
consumer protection 31
Convention on the Elimination of
   Discrimination Against Women
   (1979) (CEDAW) 3, 37, 40-42
   ESR rights *41*
   NGO action under CEDAW *42*, 48
   Optional Complaints Protocol 41
   UK compliance 41-2
Convention on the Rights of the
   Child (1989) (CRC) 43-4
   and the Children's Rights Office
      44, 48
   NGO action under the CRC 44, 48
   rights guaranteed by *44*
   UK compliance 43, 48
   UK ratification 43
Cook, Robin *21*
corporal punishment 14
Council of Europe 22, *22*, 33
   Collective Complaints Protocol 49
   NGO lobbying 6, 49
   and Protocol 12 27-8
   see also Committee of Ministers;
      European Convention on
      Human Rights; European
      Social Charter
Council of Ministers 47

courts
- assertion of civil and political rights 1
- children's participation 14
- and the ECHR 24, 28
- and ESC rights 13, *14*, 15, 28
- and European Court of Justice 32
- and a government/citizen contract 20
- and the HRA 23
- human rights case law 24, 25
- and human rights standards 7
- NGO interventions 25
- and policy decisions 3

CRC *see* Convention on the Rights of the Child
CRE *see* Commission for Racial Equality
Criminal Justice and Court Service Act *24*
Crown Court *24*
CSA *see* Child Support Agency
cultural diversity 30
cultural rights *38, 39, 41, 44*
Cyprus 35

death penalty, abolition of 24
decision making
- children's participation 14
- and the poor 8

defrauding the taxpayer 9, 19
Department of Health 44
dependants, having/not having 28
destitution: State support 25
detention
- conditions of 4, *17*, 27
- discriminatory practices 27
- without trial 8
- young offenders 24

devolution 6, 23, 28, 49
Directive Principles *16*, 17
disability 47
- disabled workers 29
- discrimination 27, 29
- and equality of opportunity 28
- integration 31
- new EU discrimination directive 4
- rights *34*

Disability Discrimination Act (1995) *24*, 25
Disability Rights Commission *24*, 27, 28, 39
discrimination
- against women 40, *41*
- disability 27, 29
- in employment *24, 35*, 37, 45
- freedom from *26*, 27
- new EU directives adopted 4
- prohibition of 2, 3, 13, 18, 25, 27-8, 33
- racial *14, 24*, 27, 29, *32*
- religious 25, 27, 29, *32*
- sex *26*, 27, 29, *34*, 40
- sexual orientation 25, 27, 29
- *see also* anti-discrimination law

dress, choice of 25
duty 19, 28

EC Treaty 32, *32*
ECHR *see* European Convention on Human Rights
ECJ *see* European Court of Justice
economic, social, and cultural rights (ESC rights)
- audits 5, 48
- economic rights 9
- education 5, 49
- enforcement in the courts 2
- as an essential foundation of citizenship 1
- examples of *11*
- historical development 11
- implementation under the HRA and anti-discrimination law 3-4
- the importance of 7
- and judges' role 3
- justiciable 2
- NGOs' role 1-2
- non-justiciability allegations 2, 10, 13-17, 28
- cost of implementation 3, 10, 16-17
- distortion of democracy 3, 10, 15
- vague and imprecisely defined 13
- variable in content 14
- political opposition to 18-20
- primacy of civil and political rights over 12-13
- progressive realisation of 3, 18
- recommendations to the ESC realm *10*
- treaties governing 2
- and the UDHR 11
- UK compliance with ESC-rights instruments 5
- use as a framework for developing UK public policy v, 1

ECOSOC *see* United Nations Economic and Social Council
EctHR *see* European Court of Human Rights
education
- asylum seekers 42-3
- children 43, *44*
- children excluded from school 4, 27, 40
- discrimination 27
- equal rights of men and women *41*
- ESC rights 5
- human rights 5
- new EU discrimination directive 4
- rights 1, 2, 7, 8, *11*, 12, 13, 15, *16*, 17, *17*, 18, 25, 28, 30, 33, *38, 39*

eligibility tests 2, 19
employment
- child labour *24, 35, 35*, 45
- contracts 29
- discrimination in *24, 35*, 37, 45
- equal opportunities and treatment *34*
- health and safety at work 2, 13, 28, 29, *39*
- information and consultation *34*
- insolvency of the employer *34*
- leave arrangements 21
- minimum age *24*, 45
- national and ethnic minorities 42
- new EU discrimination directive 4
- parental leave 29
- pay issues 2, 13, 15, 29, 31, *34, 35, 38, 39, 40*, 41, *41, 42*, 45, 48
- policy 45
- promotion *39*
- protection of disabled persons 29
- protection of pregnant workers 28
- protection of women *34*, 48
- protection of workers under the age of 18 29, 48
- redundancy *34*
- rights 8, *11*, 12, 15, *16*, 22, 28, 30, 31, 33, *34, 38, 39, 41*
- seeking 9, 19, 35, 39
- taking up work opportunities 20
- termination of *34*
- workers' representatives *34*
- working conditions 21, 29, 31, *34, 38, 39, 41*
- working time 14, 21, 29, 48

environment 47
- protection 25
- right to a healthy *16*, 22
- working 29

Equal Opportunities Commission (EOC) 27, *31*
Equal Pay Act (1970) 25
equality
- before the law 30
- between men and women 30, 40, *41*
- equal work opportunities and treatment *34*
- right to 2, 4
- sex 32
- statutory equality duty (Northern Ireland) 28

ESC rights *see* economic, social and cultural rights
ethnic minorities
- children's health 43
- discrimination against 40
- employment 42
- inner-city areas 42
- protection *43*

ethnic origin: new EU discrimination directive 4
EU *see* European Union
European Anti-Poverty Network 8
European Commission 30, 31, 32, 47
European Committee of Social Rights 33, 35, 36
European Convention on Human Rights (ECHR) 11, *17*, 39
  Additional Protocol 12 4, 5, 47
  articles reflect changing attitudes 14
  civil and political rights 7, 12, 23, 33
  complaints mechanism 33
  and the courts 24
  Fourth Protocol 37
  and the HRA 7, 23, *24*
  and human rights treaties 37
  incorporated into UK law 1, 2, 4, 9, *24*, 25
  individual petition 12
  and NGOs 24, 47
  punishment principle 4
  UK ratification of Protocol 6 *24*
  victims/potential victims of crime and abuse 16
European Court of Human Rights (EctHR) 12, 14, 16, 24, 25
European Court of Justice (ECJ) 25, 32
European Parliament 30, 32, 47
European Social Charter (1961) 3, 7, 11, 30, 33, *34*, 35
  Additional Protocol (1988) 3, 33, *34*
  Additional Protocol (1995) 5, 35, *35*, 36, 47
  and the CAJ *36*
  complaints mechanism 12, 35, *35*, 36
  focuses on ESC rights 25
  monitored by the European Social Rights Committee 22
  and NGOs 33, 35, 36, *36*, 47-8
  provisions framed in general terms *13*
  supervision 6, 33, 35
  UK compliance 35, 48
  UK ratification 22, 33, 36, 47
  see also Revised Social Charter
European Social Rights Committee 22
European Trade Union Confederation *31*
European Union (EU)
  Charter of Fundamental Rights 7, 22, 30-31, *31*
  Council of Ministers 29
  Directives 14, 29, *31*, 32, 33, 36, 43
  and ESC rights 29-30, 36
  EU law 32-3

indivisibility of human rights principle 22
  NGOs' role 1-2, 5, 29, 31-3, *31*, 32, 35-6
  and 'non-discrimination' 2
  social issues Protocol 21
  Young Workers Directive 43
European Union, Treaty of the 30
eviction 25, *26*
  arbitrary *17*
Evju, Professor Stein *13*
expression, freedom of 2, *12*, 16, 19

fair trial, right to 3, 4, *12*, 13, 14, 16, *17*
family
  definition 3
  parental responsibility 19
  protection and assistance *39*
  right to found a family 25
  right to respect for family life 3, 7, *26*
  right to social, legal, and economic protection *34*
  supporting one's 9, 19
family allowances 35
family benefits *41*
family planning *41*
Fawcett Society *42*
financial credit *41*
financial insecurity 8
Finland 35
food rights 8, *16*, 18, *39*
Foreign and Commonwealth Office
  Human Rights Annual Report (1999) *1*, 2, 7, 21, 38
  Human Rights Annual Report (2000) 7, 21, 22, 33, 47
France 17, 35
Freedom of Information Act *24*

gender
  and equality of opportunity 28
  reassignment 32
geographical location, and discrimination 27
Gingerbread *42*
Good Friday Agreement (Belfast, 1998) 22
Governmental Committee 33, 36
Greece 35
Green Paper: 'New Ambitions for our Country: A New Contract for Welfare' (1998) 19-20
Gypsy children 43

harassment *17*
  racial 43
  sexual *26*, *34*
health and safety at work 2, 13, 28, 29, *39*

health care
  asylum seekers 42
  children 43, *44*
  equal access to *41*
  high level of waiting periods for surgery 40
  rationing of 4, 27
  rights 1, 3, 8, *11*, 15, 16, *16*, 17, 22, 25, 31, *34*, 39
holidays, paid *39*
home
  loans *17*
  loss of 25
  right to respect for 7, 33
  see also housing
Home Office 24
home-school contracts 19
homelessness 40, 43
homosexuality 14, 15
House of Commons Scrutiny Select Committee 31
House of Lords European Union Committee 31
  Social Affairs, Education, and Home Affairs Sub-Committee *31*
household goods 8
housing
  repossession *26*
  rights 1, 2, 8, 13, 14, *14*, 16, *16*, 17, *17*, 18, 22, 28, 31, *34*, 39
  see also home
HRA *see* Human Rights Act
human rights
  absoluteness 14
  and the adoption of the UDHR 11
  Brazil's National Human Rights Programme 17
  and duties of the State 16, *17*
  the equal worth of all citizens 19
  the EU's commitment to 30
  and the ILO 44
  international human rights law 12, 18, 19, 20
  and the national curriculum 5
  Oxfam and JUSTICE's aim in the UK 9
  and poverty v
  and responsibilities 18-19
  seen as synonymous with civil and political rights 1
  UK government's commitment 9
  and UK law 7
  Human Rights Act (1998) (HRA) v, 1, 23-5
  civil rights v, 1, 2, 7, 23, 28, 46
  corporations and businesses 20
  courts 24
  ECHR incorporated into UK law 2, 23, *24*
  ESC rights implications 12, 25, *26*-7

Beyond Civil Rights

and the government–citizen
  relationship 1
and a Human Rights
  Commission 25
implementation 1, 4, 7, 37, 46
implementing ESC rights 3-4
and an Irish Bill of Rights 22-3
main effects of 1
NGOs' role 1, 4
Parliament 24
political rights v, 1, 2, 7, 23, 28, 46
public administration 24-5
and women's rights 41
Human Rights Commission
  Northern Ireland 2, 4, 16, *17*,
    22, *23*, 46
  proposed for UK 4, 23, 25, 46, 47
Human Rights Task Force 24-5

ICCPR *see* International Covenant
  on Civil and Political Rights
ICERD *see* International
  Convention on the Elimination
  of all Forms of Racial
  Discrimination
ICESCR *see* International Covenant
  on Economic, Social and
  Cultural Rights
ILO *see* International Labour
  Organisation
immigration, and children 43
Immigration and Asylum Act (1999)
  26
imprisonment
  for debt 37
  for fine default 3-4
India
  Constitution 12, 15, *16*
  implementation of ESC rights 17
  Supreme Court 12, *16*
indivisibility principle 7, 13, 20, 21,
  22, 28, 49
industrial action 35
information, freedom of 23
inhuman or degrading treatment
  asylum seekers *26*
  conditions of detention 27
  freedom from 7
inner-city areas 42
insecurity 8
institutional racism 27
Intergovernmental Conferences 32
International Bill of Rights 11
International Commission of Jurists iv
International Committee of Jurists *35*
International Convention on the
  Elimination of all Forms of
  Racial Discrimination (1966)
  (CERD) 3, 37, 42-3
  complaints mechanism 42
  NGO action under CERD *43*, 48

UK compliance with CERD 42-3
UK ratification 42
UK reservations to 5
International Covenant on Civil
  and Political Rights (1966)
  (ICCPR) 11, 13, 38, 39
  complaints mechanism 12
  duties and responsibilities 19
  ratification of the Second
    Optional Protocol 24
International Covenant on
  Economic, Social and Cultural
  Rights (1966) (ICESCR) 3, 7,
  11, 13, 37, 38-40
  duties and responsibilities 19
  lack of a complaints mechanism 12
  the major UN treaty protecting
    ESC rights 38
  and NGOs 5, *40*, 47-8
  Optional Protocol (proposed) 5, 47
  and progressive realisation of
    rights 18, 39
  ratification 13, 38
  rights contained in *39*
  supervision 38-9
  UK compliance 39-40
  UK reservations to 5
International Labour Conference 45
International Labour Office 45
International Labour Organisation
  (ILO)
  Committee of Experts on the
    Application of Conventions
    and Recommendations 45,
    51-2
  Conference Committee on the
    Application of Conventions
    and Recommendations 45, 52
  Conventions and
    Recommendations 3, *24*, 37,
    44-5, 52
  Governing Body 45, 52
  NGO action 48
Ireland 35
  Constitution 12, 15, *16*
  implementation of ESC rights 17
  Review Group on the
    Constitution (1996) 15, *16*
Irish Commission for Justice and
  Peace: 'Re-righting the
  Constitution' 15
Italy 17, 35

Joint Council for the Welfare of
  Immigrants *43*
judges 3, 15
JUSTICE *31*
  aim of iv
  and ECHR Additional Protocol
    12 47
  and role of NGOs 46

see also Oxfam/JUSTICE

Kenya: Constitution 21
King, William Mackenzie 13
Klug, Francesca: *Values for a Godless
  Age: The Story of the United
  Kingdom's New Bill of Rights* 12

labour inspection 45
labour law 29, 40
language
  discrimination 27
  linguistic diversity 30
  rights *44*
law reform, JUSTICE and iv
Lawrence, Stephen 27
legal aid 3, 16, *17*, *26*, 40
leisure, right to *38*, *39*, *44*
Liberty *31*, *43*
liberty, the right to *12*, 26
life, right to 7, 12, *12*, 19
lifestyle, choice of 25
Limburg Principles on the
  Implementation of the ICESCR
  18, 39
linguistic diversity 30
living conditions 29
low income 8, *17*, 23

Maastricht Guidelines on Violations
  of ESC Rights 18
Maastricht Treaty (1992) 29, 32, 39
MacGregor v UK 26
Macpherson Report 25, 27
magistrates' courts 3-4
maintenance payments 4
'margin of appreciation' principle 14
marital status 27, 28
marriage rights 25
maternity
  leave 14, *41*
  pay 35
  protecting *41*
media interests 20
MEPs *31*
migrant workers: right to protection
  and assistance *34*, 35
migration 47
minimum wage 2, 13, 15, 31
Minister for Women (UK) 24
mortgages *41*
mothers
  protection before and after
    childbirth 39
  right to social, legal, and economic
    protection *34*
  right to special care and
    assistance *38*
Mothers' Union 42
multi-national companies 20

Index

Namibia 17
National Action Plans 29-30
national curriculum 5, 49
National Minimum Wage Act (1999) 41
national minorities 42
necessities 8
negative rights 16, *17*
New Deal (Roosevelt) 13
'New Deal' schemes 39, 42
New Zealand
  Bill of Rights (1988) 12
  Constitution 12
NGOs *see* non-government organisations
Nice European Council meeting (December 2000) 29
Nigeria 17
1990 Trust *43*
non-discrimination 2, *44*
non-government organisations (NGOs)
  and Brazil's National Human Rights Programme 17
  and CERD 42, *43*
  and Committee on Economic, Social and Cultural Rights 50
  and Committee on the Elimination of Discrimination Against Women 50
  and Committee on the Elimination of Racial Discrimination 51
  and Committee on the Rights of the Child 51
  and the CRC 44
  developing advocacy on ESC rights 4-6, 46-9
    developing mechanisms for protection 4-5, 46-7
    lobbying and dissemination of information and material 5-6, 46, 48-9
    monitoring and supervision 5, 46, 47-8
    promoting ratification of key ESC rights instruments 5, 46, 47
    reviews and harmonization of domestic law and policy with international human rights standards 5, 46, 48
  developing mechanisms for protection 46-7
  and discrimination 4
  and ECHR 24, 47
  and the European Social Charter 33, 35, 36, *36*
  and HRA implementation 46, *46*
  and human rights implications of proposed legislation 24
  and intergovernmental conferences 32
  interventions in court 25, 32-3
  lobbying on ESC rights 1-2, 6, 12, 38
  monitoring and supervision 47-8
  and the 'non-discrimination' principle 2
  opportunities to promote ESC rights 1, 3, 9, 45, 46
  'Poverty Undermines Rights in the UK' submission (1997) *4*, 9, *40*
  promoting ratification of key ESC-rights instruments 47
  role in EU affairs 1-2, 5, 29, 31-3, *31*, *32*, 35-6, 47
  and the UDHR 38
  and UN instruments 37, 38-9, 42, *43*, 44, 45
Northern Ireland
  CAJ raises issues *36*
  devolution 23, 28, 49
  draft Bill of Rights 2, 8, 22-3, *23*
  Executive *23*
  Human Rights Commission 2, 4, 16, *17*, 22, *23*, 24
  poverty in 40
  promoting ESC rights in 6, 22-3, 49
  statutory equality duty 28
Northern Ireland Assembly *23*
Norway 35

occupational pension schemes 29
old-age pensions 15
older people
  abuse of 42
  rights of 30, *34*
opportunity, equality of 28, 29, *34*, *36*
Oxfam, and role of NGOs 46
Oxfam/JUSTICE: 'Poverty Undermines Rights in the UK' submission (1997) *4*, 9, *40*

P v S and Cornwall County Council 32
parents
  childraising responsibility 19
  duties re young offenders 2, 4, 26-7
Parliamentary Joint Committee on Human Rights 4, 23, 24, 25, 46-7
parliamentary sovereignty 15
pensions 15, 29
Philippines 17
Platform of European Social NGOs *31*
Plessy v. Ferguson 14
police
  acting in compliance with the ECHR 24
  and racial discrimination 27
political movements 20
political opinion 27, 28
political rights *1*
  changes over time 2-3, 14
  cost of implementation 16
  examples *12*
  and the Human Rights Act v, 1, 2, 7, 23, 28, 46
  justiciable 2
  precisely drafted 2, 13
  primacy over ESC rights 12-13
  recommendations to the civil and political realm *10*
  and the UDHR 11
Poor Law (1834) 19
Portugal 35, *35*
positive rights 16, *17*
post-natal leave 35
poverty 47
  combating 29-30, 31
  denial of full participation in society 1
  as a denial of human rights v, 1, 7-8, *23*
  deprivation of necessities 8
  'deserving'/'undeserving' poor 9
  discrimination 27
  insecurity 8
  inter-generational cycle 42
  position in the UK *40*
  poverty-reduction strategies 8
  protection against *34*
  rights/responsibilities 19, *19*
  and a social contract 9
  young women 41
'Poverty Undermines Rights in the UK' submission (1997) (Oxfam and JUSTICE) *4*, 9, *40*
pregnancy *39*, 41
private life, right to 3, 7, 13, 19, *25*, *26*
property rights 7, 15, *25*, *26*, 30, 33
protest, right of *1*
public authorities
  accountability under the Human Rights Act 1, 23-4
  adoption of international instruments 5
  and institutional racism 27
  and racial discrimination 27
  and the UNCRC 13
public health 29
public policy: development within a framework of ESC rights v, 1, 9

qualified rights 17

race
  and equality of opportunity 28
  racial discrimination *14*, *24*, 27, 29, *32*

racial equality legislation 3, *14*
racial harassment 43
racial origin 4
racism 27, *32*
Race Relations Act (1976) 25, 27, 28
Race Relations (Amendment) Act *24*, 27, *28*
Racial Relations Forum 42
Refugee Council *43*
refugees iv
rehabilitation (disabled people) *34*
religion
  discrimination 25, 27, 29, *32*
  and equality of opportunity 28
  freedom of *1*, *12*, 25, *44*
  new EU discrimination directive 4
religious diversity 30
religious movements 20
responsibilities 9, 18, 19, *19*, 20
rest, right to *38*, *39*, *44*
retirement, saving for 9, 19
Revised European Social Charter (1996) 3, *34*
  and the Charter of Fundamental Rights 31
  and NGOs 5, 36, 47, 48
  UK ratification 2, 5, 22, 33, 36, 47, 48
Robertson, G.: *Crimes Against Humanity* *14*
Robinson, Mary v, 8
Roma travellers 42
Roosevelt, Franklin D. 13

scientific advancements, right to share in *38*, *39*
Scotland
  devolution 23, 28, 49
  promoting ESC rights in 6, 49
  Scottish Executive 23
security 8, *12*
segregation *14*
self-employment 29
sex discrimination 26, 27, 29, *34*, 40
Sex Discrimination Act (1975) 25, 41
sexual harassment *26*, *34*
sexual orientation
  discrimination 25, 27, 29
  and equality of opportunity 28
  new EU discrimination directive 4
Short, Clare *21*
single parents iv
social advantage 4
social assistance 31, *34*
social contract 9
social exclusion 29, 47
  combating 29-30, 31
  denial of full participation in society 1
  as a denial of human rights 1, 7-8, 23

Northern Ireland 23
  protection against *34*
  UK government's commitment 9
Social Exclusion Unit 42
social insurance *39*, *44*
social justice 9, 13, 15, 44
social law 29
social policy
  'deserving'/'undeserving' poor 9
  duties of individuals 28
  EU competence 29
  needs-based approach 8
  rights-based approach 8
social protection 4, 33, *34*
social resettlement (disabled people) *34*
social rights *39*, 40, 49
  Northern Ireland 36
social security 35
  benefit eligibility tests 2, 19
  benefits 25, *26*, 28, 40
  children 43, *44*
  discriminatory legislation 4
  equal treatment 29
  and legal aid *26*
  new EU discrimination directive 4
  rights 1, 2, *11*, 13, 16, *16*, 31, *34*, *38*, *39*, 41
  tribunals 13
Social Security Commissioner *26*
social services: rights *14*, 31
social-welfare provision *34*, *40*, 41
society
  individual responsibility 2
  participation in 1
Soobramoney v. Minister of Health, KwaZulu Natal 15, *16*
South Africa
  Constitution 12, *16*, 17, *17*
  Constitutional Court 15, *16*
  implementation of ESC rights 17
speech, freedom of 8, *17*
standard of living 1, 2, *11*, 13, 22, *38*, *39*, *44*
Starting Line Group *32*, *32*, 36
States
  contract with the citizen 20
  and human rights 16, *17*
  and ICCPR 12
  and ICESCR 12, 14, 18
  multi-layered obligations *17*
  'negative rights' 16
  'positive rights' 16
  and progressive realisation 18
Strasbourg case law 25
subsidiarity principle 29
supply of goods, services, and cultural facilities 4
Sweden 35

tax
  discriminatory legislation 4
  exemption *26*
teenage conception 41
torture *1*, 8, *12*, *17*, 19
trade unions 49
  rights 9, *38*, *39*, 39
  Social Charter breaches 35
  status 27
Trades Union Congress *31*
training 22, 25, *34*
  disabled people *34*
  seeking 9, 19
  vocational 35, *35*
Traveller children 43
trial by jury 14
tribunals
  assertion of civil and political rights 1
  employment 13, *26*, 32
  and ESC rights *14*
  and European Court of Justice 32
  and the Human Rights Act 23
  and human rights standards 7
  and legal aid 40
  Social Security 13
tripartite consultation 45

UDHR see Universal Declaration of Human Rights
UK government
  acting in compliance with the ECHR 24
  approach to ESC rights at the European level 2, 21-2
  commitment to the promotion of human rights 7, 28
  consultation with NGOs on ESC rights 5-6, 49
  contract with citizens 19, 20
  dissemination of and debate on government reports 5, 48
  Fourth Periodic Report to the CEDAW Committee 42
  and the HRA 1, 23, 24-5, 28
  and implementation of directives 4-5
  implementing ESC rights across the UK 23
  individual responsibility emphasis 2, 2, 19
  international and domestic perspectives compared 2, 21
  and international human rights instruments 37
  legislation prohibiting discrimination 25, 27-8
  lobbying on ESC rights 1-2
  and non-compliance with ILO conventions 45
  Northern Ireland 22-3
  promotion of human rights at the national level *24*

UK Poverty Programme (UKPP) iv
unemployment *36, 38*, 39, 40, 43
United Nations (UN)
    Commission on Human Rights
        v, 11
    Convention on the Rights of the
        Child (1989) (UNCRC) 3, 13,
        14, 19, 37
    Economic and Social Council
        (ECOSOC) 50, 51
    General Assembly 7, 11, 38, 50, 51
    Refugee Convention (1951) *26*
    supervision of periodic reports
        by UN treaty-bodies 37-8
    UN Committee on Economic,
        Social and Cultural Rights
        (CESCR) 14, 18
United States
    Constitution *14*
    Supreme Court *14*
Universal Declaration of Human
    Rights (1948) (UDHR) 3, 11, *14*,
    19, 20, *21, 22*, 37, 38

civil and political rights 11, *21*, 38
    ESC rights 11, 38, *38*
unqualified rights 17

victimisation *34*
vocational guidance *34*, 35
vulnerable groups 19, 33

Wales
    devolution 23, 49
    promoting ESC rights in 6, 49
water, right to access *16*
Weiler, J.H.H. *22*
welfare state 13, 19, 20
'Welfare to Work' initiative 39
White Paper: 'Eliminating World
    Poverty: Making Globalisation
    Work for the Poor' (2000) 21
widows'/widowers' benefits *26*
women
    discrimination against 40, *41*
    right of employed women to
        protection *34*, 48

see also Convention on the
    Elimination of all Forms of
    Discrimination Against
    Women; Women's National
    Commission
Women's National Commission *42*
Women's Unit *24*
work *see* employment

xenophobia *32*

young offenders
    accommodation of young
        offenders 43
    changes in procedures for trial
        of *24*
    parents' duties 2, 4